THINGS TO CONSIDER BEFORE JESUS RETURNS

JAMES DISBROW

WestBow
PRESS
A DIVISION OF THOMAS NELSON

Scripture taken from the King James Version of the Bible.

WestBow Press books may be ordered through booksellers or by contacting:

WestBow Press
A Division of Thomas Nelson
1663 Liberty Drive
Bloomington, IN 47403
www.westbowpress.com
1 (866) 928-1240

ISBN: 978-1-4908-1890-0 (sc)
ISBN: 978-1-4908-1891-7 (e)

Library of Congress Control Number: 2013922397

Printed in the United States of America.

WestBow Press rev. date: 12/18/2013

CONTENTS

Note
Bible References:
Old Testament= OT
New Testament= NT
Young's Concordance References:
H = Hebrew
G = Greek

FOREWORD

Jesus said a prophet has no honor or respect in his own country. In fact, Jesus was barely able to work miracles in his home town due to the spirit of familiarity, which worked against his desire to bless people. Jesus also declared that traditions of men will make God's word ineffectual causing their worship to be in vain (Matthew 13:57 & Matthew 15:6-9).

The Apostle Paul preached the gospel of Jesus Christ based on personal instructions he received from the Lord. Paul was able to persuade many Jews by showing them prophecies of the Messiah in the law and the prophets. However, many Jews rejected Paul and his message. Paul was put in prison and labeled an evil doer (2Timothy 2:8-9) by the so called spiritual elite of his day. However, his destiny was great and his zeal was strong in the Lord. Paul was sent unto the Gentile nations to bring understanding concerning the kingdom of God and salvation through Jesus Christ. He preached the death, burial and resurrection of Jesus knowing that it is the blood of Jesus that brings atonement for sin and the spirit of Christ in us that completes the "new birth".

My desire is to share Jesus with the reader as Apostles Peter and Paul shared in the beginning of the church age. I pray others will read, consider and respond to the glorious gospel in truth and be obedient to the word of God. May God give light to your understanding as you read!!

A
WHO IS THE MAJORITY?

Did you ever go to a real important sports event and sit on the opposing team's side? As you began to cheer for your team, did those rooting for the opponent begin to drown you out or call you names? Did you ever feel like "the majority" always has the upper hand?

It seems as if "the majority" has the greatest momentum, and in the church world the absolute truth. This has never been the case when it comes to the numbers of people who respond to God's call.

As we look back to the "Garden of Eden", there were just 2 people, and they became separated from God due to their sin. At the time of the "Great Deluge", there were only eight people out of the entire population of the world that were saved from the flood. When God rained fire and brimstone down on Sodom and Gomorrah, there were just 4 people that were saved out of the cities, and one of them was destroyed due to her desire to be with "the majority" back in that sinful environment.

When Jesus was ministering here on earth, he had 12 disciples, and one of them betrayed him. At the Mount of Transfiguration, Jesus had just 3 disciples with him, and sadly, when Jesus went to the cross there was only one disciple there.

"The majority" believe they have the corner on truth as they convincingly proclaim their view points on biblical subjects. Do we really think that because current or popular beliefs are supported by the multitude in Christendom what they declare is gospel?

Jesus Christ said that entrance into the Kingdom of God is through a narrow opening. This statement has spiritual application. He lets us know that there is a wide gate and broad way that will lead us to destruction (carnal reasoning and living will destroy us). Sadly, he says *many* will chose this path for their lives! Jesus emphasized that it is a strait gate and a narrow way that leads us unto eternal life. He proclaimed *few* people will find everlasting life (Mat 7:13-14)!

Many will choose the broad way because of its glamour, hype and many social attractions. Just like New York City, people are drawn to the "Broadway" because there is much excitement, entertainment and a false sense of security.

We learn in the study of the scripture that God's word is not pleasant to the flesh, neither is it popular to the carnal mindset. We find out that we have to suffer with Jesus if we want to reign with him in his kingdom (2 Timothy 2:12). All who live Godly in Christ Jesus will suffer persecution (2 Timothy 3:12), but still we are to present our bodies as living sacrifices, holy and acceptable unto God, which is our reasonable service as Christians (Romans 12:1). Further, we are assured that if we do not allow peace and holiness to be our way, we will not see the Lord (Hebrews 12:14)!

These are just a few scriptures that bring us down to reality. We must study to show ourselves approved unto God (2 Timothy 2:15), and believe God's word in the face of tradition even though it may have been taught for centuries.

On the Mount of Olives, before Jesus would go to Jerusalem and be killed, he spoke to his disciples and charged them not to be deceived. This is why we must consider many things!

Chapter 1

SAVING FAITH IS?

The Bible tells us that without faith it is impossible to please God (Hebrews 11:6). If this is true, it is essential that we understand what God's kind of faith looks like. We must examine biblical faith to see if our faith is truly what God is looking for in us.

One might ask where we would look to find an example of faith that saves. Who has exhibited faith that has pleased God? The bible gives us many illustrations! The Apostle Paul referred to Abraham as the "father of faith" (Romans 4:16), and a close examination of Abraham's obedience to God will help us understand the God kind of faith.

First, let's look at a dictionary's definition of faith. One example in the Merriam-Webster Dictionary states that faith is a firm belief in something for which there is no proof. Hebrews 11:1 gives us a similar definition:

> Hebrews 11:1 Now faith is the substance of things hoped for, the evidence of things not seen.

Hebrews 1:1 declares that faith exists as the assurance or guarantee of things earnestly expected, having the proof or verification of that which is anticipated, though we have not yet seen its manifestation. This kind of faith can be seen in the life of Abraham.

Abraham was a Chaldean, a member of an ancient Semitic people that became dominant in Babylonia. His name was originally Abram. We begin to read about his life in Genesis chapters 11 and 12. We have no real information related to Abram's history or relationship with God prior to Genesis 12:1-2. God instructs Abram to leave his country and his people and go to a country that He would show him. God promises that He would bless Abram and build a great nation through Abram and his family. **Abram's response to God's command proved his faith in God.** The Bible says at 75 years old Abram left his home in Haran and took his wife Sarai, and Lot his brother's son, and all their substance that they had gathered, and the souls that they had gotten in Haran; and they went forth to go into the land of Canaan (Genesis 12:5). What an amazing example of courage and faith that in those days, without all the modern conveniences of travel or shipping, Abram would uproot his life and travel hundreds of miles on foot with all that he possessed. Abram and Sarai had to break ties with friends, and possibly close family members, as well as organize a trip to an unknown land. Abram followed God's instructions based on God's spoken word, Genesis 12:1.

The scripture lets us know that Sarai was barren, having been unable to bare children for Abram (Genesis 11:30). In Genesis 13:16, God is still telling Abram that He would make his seed as the dust of the earth. How was God going to fulfill His promise and bless the nations of the world through Abram, seeing he was old and having no offspring? We should understand that with God all things are possible (Matthew 19:26 and Mark 10:27)! There is much more to Abram's story, but our focus here continues to be Abram's faith.

Abram was 86 years old when he had a son through Sarai's servant Hagar (Genesis 16:16). This is an example of trying to make God's promises come to reality through our own works or abilities. The promised seed was to be Abram's son through Sarai, *not* Hagar. Ishmael was born of Hagar, but the promised seed or offspring was to be Isaac by Sarai.

At 99 years old, God reaffirms the covenant with Abram and changes his name to Abraham (Genesis 17:1). Sarai's name is also changed to Sarah (Genesis

17:15). In verse #17, Abraham laughs at the thought that God would give him a son at 100 years old or that Sarah could bare a child at 90. But Sarah does conceive, delivers a son and they name him Isaac (Genesis 21:1-3).

This information lets us known that from the age of 75, when God told Abram/Abraham that he would bring forth a great nation out of his loins (Genesis 12:2), to the time Sarah delivers her child of promise was 25 years. Abraham believed God all those years and continued with his wife, keeping the hope alive that Sarah would conceive and the promise of God would be fulfilled.

Some time passed and God would test Abraham's faith once again. God's instructions came to Abraham and he had to choose his will or God's word. What God was about to tell Abraham had to have fallen heavily upon his heart. God told Abraham to take his son to the mountain of Moriah and offer him there as a sacrifice (Genesis 22:2). Abraham did not take long to make that faithful decision; the next morning preparations were made and they left to fulfill the will of God.

We know something obvious about Isaac at this point. Isaac was not a baby and he probably wasn't a *young* lad because Abraham took the wood of the burnt offering, and laid it upon Isaac his son to carry up the mountain (Genesis 22:6). We should understand that Isaac was to be a burnt offering upon an altar Abraham was instructed to build. Imagine killing your child, no matter how long you waited for it to be born, and then burning the body of that child! That was God's instruction and Abraham's intention as he and his son climbed up the mountain.

Isaac questioned his father by asking him where the lamb was that they were to sacrifice. Abraham's response was remarkable as he affirmed to Isaac that God would provide the sacrifice (Genesis 22:8). Abraham had previously experienced something great with God, and he knew if he had to take Isaac's life, God would (not just could) raise him from the dead. Abraham said something very telling when he told his servants to stay with the donkey, that the lad and he will go and worship, and then they would come back to them later (Genesis 22:5). Abraham had faith that God was in control, and that if he was obedient God would fulfill the promise made that Isaac would be a blessing to the nations!

Scripture says that they came to the place which God had told him of; and Abraham built an altar there. He laid the wood in order, bound his son, and laid him on the altar upon the wood. As Abraham stretched forth his hand, and took the knife to slay his son, an angel of the LORD called unto him out of heaven and said, Abraham lay not your hand upon the lad, neither do anything unto him. Now I know that you fear God, seeing you have not withheld your only son (Genesis 22:9-12).

Abraham lifted up his eyes and saw behind him a ram caught in a dense growth of bushes by his horns. Abraham freed the ram and offered him up for a burnt offering instead of his son. Abraham called the name of that place Jehovahjireh, which means "the Lord will see to it" or "will provide" (Genesis 22:13-14)!

We briefly examined 2 separate instances where God gave Abram/ Abraham personally difficult directives to obey. Consider, however that with the commandments given there were also promises attached. This wasn't like a mean ole king showing his power over his subject. This was the Creator making a covenant with a man, who if he was faithful, would bring forth a blessing to all mankind. The promise of God that Abraham's seed would bring blessings to mankind was prophetic and specifically spoke of Jesus Christ (Galatians 3:16)!

There is much more to learn about Abraham's life, which is a good study for another time. Continuing to look at and understand the kind of faith that pleases God, the Apostle Paul writes about Abraham's faith in the 4th chapter of the book of Romans, which gives us a deeper understanding of "Saving Faith".

Examining Abraham's response to God's instructions, would someone think that Abraham was justified by *what* he did or by the reason *why* he did the things he was told to do? If Abraham was made right by the things he did, he would have a reason to boast in himself alone. Apostle Paul wrote that Abraham *believed*

God, and it was counted unto him for righteousness (Romans 4:3). Abraham's confidence in God caused him to obey God by doing the things commanded. **It was corresponding action to God's directives, or simple obedience on Abraham's part, that revealed the faith in God that he already possessed.** If Abraham had not obeyed God, his faith would have been considered to be nonexistent from God's perspective. James makes this very clear!

> James 2:21-22 Was not Abraham our father justified by works, when he had offered Isaac his son upon the altar? (22) Seest thou how faith wrought (worked together) with his works (doing), and by works (doing) was faith made perfect (complete)? James 2:26 For as the body without the spirit is dead, so faith without works (corresponding action to God's word) is dead also. (Author's words are in parenthesis.)

We should remember that the promise that Abraham should be the heir of the world, was not to Abraham, or to his seed, through the law, but through the righteousness of faith (Romans 4:13). We see then that Abraham had deeply planted in his heart (mind and emotions) the assurance that God would give him a son; and through that son, all the nations or ethnic groups in the world would be blessed. All the promises of God were not fulfilled in Abraham's time, but he could picture them in his mind fulfilled (proof), causing him to obey. The confirmation of the promises being fulfilled was Abraham's knowledge of God. Abraham believed God and knew that God would reward his faith.

Both Paul and James wrote that righteousness was imputed or accounted to Abraham because he believed God (Romans 4:3, Galatians 3:6 and James 2:3). Faith brought Abraham into right standing with God.

Romans chapter 4 gives a good breakdown as to what qualified Abraham's faith to be acceptable with God. When there appeared to be no hope that Sarah could bear a child, Abraham kept his expectation up, that he might become the father of many nations, according to that which God had spoken! Abraham considered not their bodies, which were well past the age of child bearing. They continued in their attempts to procreate until Sarah conceived! Abraham was one hundred years old and Sarah was ninety when Isaac was born. Abraham was not astonished or bowled over by what God had promised to the point of unbelief, but was strong in faith, giving glory to God! Like Abraham, the place we should all come to in our walk with God is that we are fully persuaded that, what God has promised in His word, God is able also to perform (Romans 4:17-22)! Apostle Paul lets us know that this is the faith level that Abraham had risen to in his relationship with his Creator!

When we have come to this level in our faith walk where God tells us what he wants us to do and we do it trusting Him, we have embraced the faith of father Abraham!

Faith must be understood to be more than just a verbal or even a sincere prayer. The Bible says we are saved by grace through, or by the means of, faith (Ephesians 2:8). But remember also that faith comes by the hearing of the word of God (Romans 10:17). The word "hearing" is the Greek word *ak-o-ay'* (G189), which implies through its root word "to understand" (G191). It does no good to just hear the sound without the meaning of the words spoken! We must comprehend God's word before saving faith can be produced. The word of God impacts our thought processes and enters into our hearts. Through this process a decision is made! We will either reject God's good word, or we will be obedient to His word proving our faith!

God wants us to understand that obedience is better than sacrifice? This is not just an outdated OT scripture!

> 1 Samuel 15:22-23 And Samuel said, Hath the LORD as great delight in burnt offerings and sacrifices, as in obeying the voice of the LORD? Behold, <u>to obey is better than sacrifice</u>, and to hearken than the fat of rams. (23) For rebellion is as the sin of witchcraft, and stubbornness is as iniquity and idolatry. Because <u>thou hast rejected the word of the LORD,</u> <u>he hath also rejected thee</u> from being king.

The component of faith that is often missed today is the doing of God's will! As previously mentioned, James wrote concerning the doing of God's word. He is frankly telling us that faith without works (the doing of God's word) renders our faith dead (James 2:20 & 26)! We must receive God's word, consider it closely, understand it and <u>do it</u>! This is the kind of faith pleasing to God that He is looking to find in each one of us, which will bring us to salvation!

Many who went to Sunday School as a children know that Jesus taught in parables. We must consider the things that he taught which are recorded in the gospels (Matthew, Mark, Luke and John). In the 13th chapter of Matthew, Jesus refers to the word of God as "seed". We know the optimal outcome of good seed planted in good ground is good fruit! Jesus likens the heart, or mind, of a person as the ground, or the soil that the seed, God's word, is to be planted into (Matthew 13:4-8).

Jesus said a sower went forth to sow, and some seeds fell by the way side, and the fowls came and devoured the seed. Some seed fell upon stony or rocky ground where there wasn't a depth of soil. Right away when the seed produced life through the soil, the sun scorched it because there wasn't a good root system and it withered away. Some seed fell among thorns. The thorns sprung up and choked the life being produced. There was other seed, which fell into good ground, and brought forth much fruit (some a hundredfold, some sixtyfold, some thirtyfold). Jesus explained these previous verses:

Matthew 13:18-23 Hear ye therefore the parable of the sower. (19) When any one heareth the word of the kingdom, and understandeth it not, then cometh <u>the wicked one, and catcheth away that which was sown in his heart</u>. This is he which received seed by <u>the way side</u>. (20) But he that received <u>the seed into stony places</u>, the same is he that heareth the word, and anon with joy receiveth it; (21) Yet hath he not root in himself, but dureth for a while: for when <u>tribulation or persecution ariseth because of the word, by and by he is offended</u>. (22) He also that received <u>seed among the thorns</u> is he that heareth

7

the word; and <u>the care of this world, and the deceitfulness of riches, choke the</u> <u>word</u>, and he becometh unfruitful. (23) But he that received seed into the <u>good</u> <u>ground</u> is he that heareth the word, and understandeth it; which also <u>beareth</u> <u>fruit</u>, and bringeth forth, some an hundredfold, some sixty, some thirty.

In this parable Jesus, is telling us that the enemy will quickly steal God's word from us if our minds are not in a place to receive it. Seed sown on hard ground never takes root. Similarly, when God's word lands on a hardened heart, it does not enter their belief system. Satan is right there with worldly influences to steal the word while we think on our own desires.

Some people will embrace God's word for a time. However, the truth of the word never becomes planted deep into their hearts to really take root. When opposition and troubles comes their way because they have taken a stand on the word of God, many will take offense and become discouraged. Offense and discouragement often makes a person give up their hope.

Most people's lives are full of distractions. There are things in our lives, if we are not careful, that will take our thoughts and desires away from the "Kingdom of God". When God's word becomes stunted within us, due to the concerns of life and materialism, we lose our focus and we become fruitless.

The good news is that God's word does find rich soil. Good hearts are plowed and able to receive. These are minds that are open to God and His will. These hearts produced much fruit through faith in the word of God!

Apostle Paul wrote that those who have obeyed the gospel of Jesus Christ through faith are the children of Abraham. They have been justified through faith and are blessed with faithful Abraham. Paul also lets us know that no man is justified by the law in the sight of God for, **The just shall live by faith**. He writes that the law is not of faith: but, "The man that doeth them shall live in them (Galatians 3:7-12)".

The person who believes they must keep the many tenets of the "Mosaic Law", or somehow by doing "good works" is justified before God, has missed the value of the "Cross of Christ"! Attempts to be right before God by keeping the law requires that the individual give themselves wholly to each duty prescribed as is stated in Leviticus 18:5. The problem is that no man is able to keep the whole law. Apostle Paul wrote, "by the deeds of the law there shall no flesh be justified in God's sight: for by the law is the knowledge of sin" (Romans 3:20).

Jesus, and his victory on the cross, is the focus of our Christian faith. Apostle Paul stated that he preached Christ crucified (1 Corinthians 1:23) and further declared that he counted all things as a loss for the outstanding and marvelous knowledge of Christ Jesus his Lord (Philippians 3:8). This great apostle traveled to the city of Corinth proclaiming the word of God. Paul was resolute, unwavering in his mind, that he would consider sharing nothing but Jesus Christ crucified (1 Corinthians 2:2)!

"Saving Faith" starts with believing that Jesus died to give us the opportunity to be right with God. Each of us must seize the "Grace of God" through Jesus Christ by believing in Jesus' sacrifice on the cross, and then applying it to our lives. The application of the blood of Christ is a step in faith!! The 1st message preached on the day the "New Covenant" began was by the Apostle Peter. Jesus told Peter he would give him the keys to the kingdom of heaven, and what he bound or loosened on earth would be done similarly in heaven (Matthew 16:16-19). In other words, Jesus has given Peter the words of truth that will unlock heaven's door and eternal life for us, if we believe God's words through Peter and allow faith to have its perfect work like Abraham! Peter preached Jesus of Nazareth crucified and raised from the dead, giving the people understanding that God had made Jesus both Lord and Christ (Acts 2:14-36).

Many of those hearing the gospel became convicted by the word of God and asked what they should do. They were told that everyone needed to repent, and be baptized in the name of Jesus Christ for the remission of sins (Acts 2:38). They were assured that they would receive the gift of the Holy Ghost: Pure Life! Jesus told Nicodemus, a Pharisee, "you must be born again" (John 3:3-8). We are "born again" when we receive new life, the Holy Spirit! Peter said that the Holy Spirit

(Ghost) is promised to all that are afar off (even now), even as many as the Lord our God shall call (Acts 2:39). In obedience to the word of God preached, 3,000 souls were born again that very day. They repented; they were baptized in Jesus' name; and they received "New Life"!

> Acts 2:41 Then they that gladly received (good ground) his word were baptized (responsive to God's word-*not* works based on self will): and the same day there were added unto them about <u>three thousand souls</u>.

Considering Abraham's responses to the word of God, by obeying the directives given and thereby having righteousness imputed to him, what should our response be to the gospel preached at the beginning of the church age? Faith that saves is more than a sincere prayer!

Chapter 2

THE CROSS

What did God know, and when did he know it? When a tragic event happens that affects the lives of many people, usually the questions asked by the authorities in charge are, "what did they know, and when did they know it". God is the ultimate authority, and concerning the sin of Adam or the death of Jesus Christ, He was not caught off guard!

The word of God tells us that known unto God are all his works from the beginning of the world (Acts 15:18). In fact, Isaiah asks the following questions:

> Isaiah 40:12-14 Who hath measured the waters in the hollow of his hand, and meted out heaven with the span, and comprehended the dust of the earth in a measure, and weighed the mountains in scales, and the hills in a balance? <u>Who hath directed the Spirit of the LORD, or being his counsellor hath taught him</u>? With whom took he counsel, and who instructed him, and taught him in the path of judgment, and taught him knowledge, and shewed to him the way of understanding?

These are rhetorical questions of course. In Genesis 1:1 we read that in the beginning God created the heavens and the earth. In John 1:1 we read, in the beginning was *"the word"* (reasoning, intellect or plan) and "the word" was with "God" (a noun) and the word was "god" (an adjective meaning godly or divine). Check an "Interlinear Translation" Greek/English for clarity. This information lets us know that God has been working His plan to fulfillment. God's plan centers around Jesus of Nazareth, whom God has made both Lord and Christ (Acts 2:36). Jesus Christ was not plan "B" in case Adam failed! We must understand that God has designed this creation with foreknowledge of its final outcome. He knows our thoughts, motives and actions before they are conceived in our own minds. God is omniscience, he's not just smart! God knows everything before it happens! God knew Adam's mental, emotional and spiritual make up, and before it happened, God knew Adam and Eve would eat of the "Tree of the Knowledge of Good and Evil".

In Genesis 1:27 we read that "God created man in his own image[1], in the image of God created he him[2]; male and female created he them"[3]. God created mankind as [1]spirit beings, [2]giving us an intellect with the faculty to make decisions and create. God created mankind [3]male and female for the purpose of procreation, to populate the earth.

Genesis 1:31 says that God saw everything that he had made, and, behold, it was very good. It must be understood that God created everything the way He wanted it, to please Himself, and to fulfill His desired objectives! We must also realize that God created us with the ability to think, and to make our own conclusions and decisions, including Adam. We have intellect that enables us to discern and to react based upon our experiences and other information.

God formed man of the dust of the ground, and breathed into his nostrils the breath of life; and man became a living soul (Genesis 2:7). Adam was placed by God in the "Garden of Eden", a place of protection and pleasure. God took a rib from Adam's side and made him a "help meet" (Eve), someone to aid him in life who was a counterpart to himself, a female (opposite sex).

God gave Adam the responsibility to work the garden and to care for it. Adam was told that he could eat of every tree in the garden except for the "Tree of the Knowledge of Good and Evil". He was warned that if he ate the fruit from that tree, he would die that very day (Genesis 2:16-17)! This was the only known or recorded law that Adam had been given by God. We see in the text that the serpent came to tempt Eve. Eve repeats the warning in her discussion with the serpent, knowing full well what God had said would happen!

Did God know that Adam and Eve would eat fruit from that forbidden tree? Another rhetorical question! The serpent told Eve that if she ate the fruit from that tree, she wouldn't surely die (Genesis 3:4). Satan is still telling mankind, "You Won't Surely Die!" Unfortunately for Adam, Eve and all of us, she not only ate of the "Tree of the Knowledge of Good and Evil", but she gave it to her husband, and he ate! The result of their action caused them to be removed from the "Garden of Eden" that very day (Genesis 3:23). Their disobedience brought about a spiritual death, separating them from the presence of God. They became dead in trespasses and sins. Adam lived to be 930 years old, and then he physically died (Genesis 5:5).

The Apostle Peter wrote that one day is with the Lord as a thousand years, and a thousand years as one day (2 Peter 3:8). This is confirmed in Psalms 90:4, "For a thousand years in thy sight are b*ut* as yesterday when it is past, and *as* a watch in the night".

The very day Adam and Eve ate the "Forbidden Fruit", they were removed from God's presence, suffering spiritual death. This judgment of spiritual death was passed down to Adam and Eve's descendants. Adam's children, all of humanity, are born into the earth with the judgment of death upon them. The judgment of spiritual and physical death has come upon all humanity through the disobedience of Adam and Eve. Adam did not live to be 1,000 years old. God kept His word!

Why would God make Adam and Eve, put them in His place of protection, and then allow a serpent (the tempter) to come into the garden? Remember, God gave them 1 law, don't eat from that tree! The tempter was there to deceive, forcing Adam and Eve to make a decision. Their decision touches our lives every day. Will we obey God or believe the enemy? We all have decisions we are faced with every day, which cause us to choose good or evil (God or self). Either we choose God or we disregard His help and provision.

God knew what he had put in Adam. Adam and Eve were flesh, powerless to the lust that was part of their makeup (DNA). Eve saw that the tree was good for food (lust of the flesh), and that it was pleasant to the eyes (lust of the eyes), and a tree to be desired to make one wise (pride of life). Genesis 3:6 lets us know that Eve's desire and reasoning responded to her flesh nature causing her to give in to the temptation. Adam, also knowing the consequences, acted upon his flesh and his wife's desire for him to eat the forbidden fruit. God knew what they would do and made provision for mankind's redemption!

Apostle Peter wrote that the true church is redeemed with the precious blood of Christ, who was <u>foreordained</u> (G4267 ordain or order before) <u>before the foundation</u> (G2602 founding or conception) <u>of the world</u>, but was manifest in these last times for us, who by him do believe in God (1 Peter 1:18-21). Revelation 13:8 refers to the book of life of <u>the Lamb slain from the foundation of the world</u>. Both of these scriptures let us know that in the foreknowledge and will of God, Jesus' death on the cross was purposed by Him before the creation was spoken into being!

Jesus Christ is the remedy for sin! The condemnation upon humanity due to Adam and Eve's sins is removed only through the finished work of the cross. We must take note of Apostle Paul's writing in the book of Ephesians. Paul tells the church that God has chosen the saints (the true church) in Jesus Christ before the foundation of the world, having predestinated them unto the adoption of children by Jesus Christ to himself, according to the good pleasure of his will (Ephesians 1:4-6). God's "church" are those who have responded to the gospel. They are those who came out of the world system and who are set apart for the kingdom of God through the death, burial and resurrection of Jesus Christ. Their destiny, promised in Christ, was seized upon when the sacrifice of Jesus on the cross was applied to their lives.

In 1 Corinthians 1:18, Apostle Paul states that the preaching of the cross is to them that perish foolishness; but unto us which are saved it is the power of God. The cross must be preached today so souls can choose life. People need to hear the gospel, consider the instructions given through the apostles' words and have an opportunity to respond. Jesus is ready to reconcile Jew and Gentile both unto God in one body through what he accomplished on the cross. Jesus is able to eliminate the hostility caused by sin (Ephesians 2:16) and set us right with God.

Jesus suffered the physical pain of the cross as well as the emotional disgrace and humiliation of being made an example of sin. The scripture says Jesus was made to be sin for us, who knew no sin; that we might be made the righteousness of God in him (2 Corinthians 5:21). He despised the shame of being hung out for the world to curse and ridicule, but he endured (Hebrews 12:2).

The cross of Christ is, to us, the perfect example of faith toward God. After Jesus shared the last supper with his disciples, he went up to the Mount of Olives to pray, his disciples following him. Jesus told them to pray, and he separated himself from them about a "stone's throw away". Jesus became very troubled while praying and said to God, "Father, if thou be willing, remove this cup from me: **nevertheless not my will, but thine, be done."** Jesus was in agony as he prayed with much more seriousness. Jesus sweat profusely enough that apparently his sweat became infused with blood and saturated the ground around him (Luke 22:39-44).

Jesus knew what his crucifixion would entail as the Romans carried out death sentences by nailing the condemned prisoners' feet to a stake and their hands to a cross beam. Those crucified would die a painful death, and to make sure the victims were dead, Roman soldiers would break their legs. Jesus knew it was his destiny to offer himself as a sacrifice for sin. The bible says that because of the joy that he had in knowing what his faith would bring, Jesus endured the death on the cross for all of humanity (Hebrews 12:2). Jesus believed God's word and knew that he would be raised from the dead. I am sure he saw the hope of immortality and the ability to bring others to right standing with God.

The cross is a picture of perfect love. God so loved the world; He gave his very best, His only begotten son (John 3:16). We also need to consider the abundant love of Jesus Christ who allowed the horrific torture upon himself that we could be freed from the condemnation of sin! Romans 5:7-10 forces each of us to consider the truth, that it's hard to find someone who will give his or her life for another person. The scripture continues by saying that perhaps for a good man someone would courageously give their life. But God introduced or showed us the love He provided for us, in that, while we were yet sinners, His anointed, Christ Jesus, died for us. Because of Jesus' death on the cross, we can now be justified by his blood; we can be saved from God's wrath through Christ. We can be reconciled to God by the death of his Son, and we can be victorious through his life in us.

The cross of Christ is a symbol of love. We do not hang an empty cross in our sanctuaries as an object of worship, but it is a constant reminder that everything God has provided for us is accessed by the love of Christ who died upon an "old rugged cross". God will supply all our needs according to his riches in glory by Christ Jesus (Philippians 4:19). The great provisions given to us by God are acquired only due to Jesus' obedience to God and his love realized at the cross!

Chapter 3

FINDING GOD THROUGH HIS ANOINTED

I am reminded of a song that was popular some years ago that lamented the time lost looking for love in all the wrong places. Men and women alike are still looking in places they shouldn't to find acceptance, compassion and comfort. In most relationships, if a person feels like they belong, that they are treated considerately and that they have reassurance their bond with the other person is solid, they are put at ease.

Statistically, however, approximately half of the marriages that are performed in America are broken by infidelity or a loss of passion and end up in divorce. This is also true in the American church. So there is no guarantee that the person you thought was your "soul mate" will be with you to the end. This is tragic but true.

God is love, so if you are looking for love in the right place, you will find it where you find Jehovah, the Eternal Himself! The God of Abraham, Isaac and Jacob is identified in the scriptures as love (1 John 4:16). The bible defines God as a spirit, a consuming fire, but it is important to know Him as love! In God we will find acceptance, benevolence and comfort. God has passion for us all!

The way to God is found in knowing Jesus Christ, who is the express image of God's love (Hebrews 1:3). Jesus said that the only way to the Father was through him (John 14:6). We must first connect with Jesus, God's anointed son. There is a path, that if followed, will lead us all to God. It is the plan of God that has been laid out for us in the New Testament. The apostles of Jesus Christ were commissioned by Jesus to go into the world and direct people to his cross. We are not to focus on that wooden stake and cross bar that held Jesus as he died. It is the finished work of the cross that must be understood and seized upon by each of us. The book of Revelation speaks of Jesus as a lamb slain from the foundation of the world (Revelation 13:8). We know from historians and from the bible itself that Jesus died about 2,000 years ago. Jesus did not die before the world was spoken into being by God. This reveals the forethought concerning Jesus in God's mind! God's plan called for something very hard for mankind to understand, the death of His son! In God's plan, miracles could and would occur because of Jesus Christ's death on the cross and through his glorious resurrection! Jesus' blood sacrifice would be the atonement for sin once his blood was applied to a believer's life!

God's will concerning Jesus' earthly ministry was fulfilled, and mankind's opportunity for redemption had been realized upon Jesus' death, burial and resurrection. The human race has been given access back into the "GRACE" of God. Jesus always had a desire to be obedient to God's will and to His purpose (John 8:29). Scripture tells us that it was because of the exceeding joy in Jesus' heart that he was able to endure the crucifixion (Hebrews 12:2). That joy in Jesus' heart must have been the countless numbers of souls that would find their way to God through his faithfulness.

God gave Israel the Mosaic Law (God's law given through Moses) and in those ordinances were rough images (types and shadows) showing us how we can approach the throne of God (Hebrews 10:1)! The "Tabernacle in the Wilderness" is a revealing study with its furnishings and it gives us both reassurance and a greater understanding how we may reach the throne of God!

Looking at the tabernacle you would have seen a walled perimeter around the activities taking place within the area known as the outer court (Exodus chapter 27). Outside of the walled perimeter we have a picture of the world. The world does not know what is going on inside the church. Jesus was resolute when he said that unless a person has been born again that individual cannot see and neither can they enter the kingdom of God (John 3:3-5). Jesus was saying that a person has to be born from above, or regenerated spiritually, before they will understand the things of God's kingdom. An individual has to be born again to enter into fellowship with the household of God.

There is an opening or gate (Exodus 27:16), which allows access into to the "Outer Court" of the walled perimeter. This gate reminds us that Jesus is the "door" (G2374 or gate) into the sheepfold (John 10:1). The sheepfold is defined as a courtyard or place of well-being or protection. We see right away that the starting point on our journey to the throne of God starts with Jesus opening the way!

The first object a person will see when entering the walled perimeter is the "Brazen Altar". Those approaching the worship of God are always required to bring a sacrifice. The children of Israel would bring their offerings of bulls and goats that would be burnt upon the brazen or bronze altar. In the New Covenant the first offering we bring on our way to the presence of God is ourselves. We put ourselves upon the altar of sacrifice, which is repentance for our sins and our inability to please God. A time of reflection upon God's word should cause a person to give up self with a heart toward doing the will of God in their lives. Repentance is not just saying, "I'm sorry"' but a sincere desire to do the will of God in our lives. Repentance is in fact death to our own desires and will. We learn that all true worship of God demands a sacrifice. The "Brazen Altar" is a type or shadow of Jesus' sacrifice on the cross and our repentance!

The Old Testament seems to connect brass or bronze with sin, judgment and forgiveness. In the book of Numbers 21:6-9 we see the judgment of God on the children of Israel for their much complaining. God sent fiery serpents to bite the people for their ill-tempered griping and many died. Moses prayed to God on behalf of God's people and because of God's love He provided a remedy for their sin. Moses followed God's instruction and made a serpent out of bronze. The bronze serpent was then put on a pole and raised up in the air so the people could see it. When anyone would look upon the bronze serpent they would live. This is also a shadow of the gospel being preached (John 3:14)!

In the "Outer Court" we see another bronze object. Before the priests would be able to go into the tented area called the "Holy Place" they had to wash at the "Brazen Laver". Before we come to God through Christ Jesus we are under condemnation for sin and we are without God's blessing of salvation (Ephesians 2:11-13). Washing at the brazen laver or basin is a picture of New Testament baptism. As we come to understand that the Tabernacle in the Wilderness is a picture of Jesus bringing us to God we can clearly see that Christian baptism is in Jesus' name!

In the outer court we have seen the brazen altar and the brazen laver. Both of these items deal with the flesh or human nature. Unfortunately many people who have repented and were baptized in Jesus' name never progress any further in their quest to find God. They remain worldly in the way they think and in the things they do. It would be like the priests wandering around outside of the tented area of the tabernacle and never entering the Holy Place!

Once we have repented of our sins and have been baptized in Jesus' name we have the promise of the Holy Spirit. The priests having offered sacrifices on the "Brazen Altar" and having washed at the "Brazen Laver" can enter the "Holy Place". Following Apostle Peter's instructions of repenting and being baptized in Jesus' name, we have the promise of the Holy Spirit (Acts 2:38-39). The Holy Spirit is our Holy Place where we really come alive and mature as Christians.

Inside the Holy Place there are 3 pieces of furniture that we will see. On the left a candlestick with 7 branches, on the right side of the room is a table of showbread, and at the end of the room near a large curtain or veil is the altar of incense. These 3 pieces of furniture all represent the work of the Spirit, which is Christ in us, the hope of glory (Colossians 1:27).

The 7 branch golden candlestick is a picture of Christ Jesus the light of the world (John 8:12) bringing enlightenment to humanity throughout the 7 church ages. Jesus discusses the 7 churches in the book of Revelation chapters 2 and 3. The 7 churches consist of people who had been called out of the world and should have been demonstrating the righteousness of God through the Holy Spirit, Jesus

Christ himself living in the believer. Oil in the lamp fills the 7 tubes or branches of the golden candlestick. When the oil is lit a golden glow reflects from the golden candlestick lighting up the dark tented Holy Place. This is a picture of the Holy Spirit in the church shining brightly in a dark world. It is the life of Jesus Christ living and working in the believer!

The table of show bread reminds us that Jesus is the bread of life (John 6:48). The table was made of acacia wood and overlaid with pure gold. Jesus was made the seed of David according to the flesh, but declared to be the son of God by the spirit of holiness (Romans 1:3-4). We can see a spiritual application where the inexpensive wood (flesh) is covered by precious gold (Spirit of God). The attending priests would bake bread with fine flour and allow the 12 loaves of bread to remain on the table before the Lord for one week. Every Sabbath the priests would remove the bread and eat it in the Holy Place just as the word of God is consumed by the church in heavenly places (Ephesians 1:3)! We look back at the "Last Supper" and see the 12 disciples at the table with Jesus. Jesus said for them to take and eat the unleavened bread and in the future they should eat in remembrance of his body which was given for them (Luke 22:19). The "Showbread" was called "bread of the presence" because it was always to be in God's presence. The church is before Jesus at all times and the bread of life is in them!

The last item of furniture in the "Holy Place" is the "Altar of Incense" (Exodus 30:1-8). The "Altar of Incense" was also made of acacia wood and covered with fine gold giving us the same example or testimony of Christ. Aaron was to burn sweet incense upon the altar. In Revelation 5:8 the Apostle John wrote that the prayers of the saints were likened to odors and also in Revelation 8:4 that the prayers of the saints will ascend up before God. The church, those who are "called out" from the world system into the kingdom of God, are being made kings and priests unto God (Revelation 1:6 and Revelation 5:10). The church is therefore called to prayer, that we should pray for one another and that we should pray fervently in righteousness (James 5:16)! Jesus is our example when it comes to our prayer life. Many times he had to separate himself from others (Matthew 14:23) and others from himself so his prayers would not be hindered (Matthew 9:25). The "Altar of Incense" represents the prayer life of Jesus and those who are his!

Here we are standing at the veil or curtian that separates the "Holy of Holies" from the "Holy Place". Under the "Mosaic Law" only the high priest could go beyond the veil into the "Holy of Holies". He could only go in to that area of the tabernacle once a year. The high priest would enter with the exact blood sacrifice God had instructed him to bring. He would offer the blood upon the "Mercy Seat", which was on top of the "Ark of the Covenant".

The veil was very thick and had "Cherubims" woven upon it. Cherubims are not grown up Cherubs or little baby looking angels. Looking back in time we remember the story of Adam and Eve who were escorted out of the "Garden of Eden" for disobeying God. God placed Cherubims with flaming swords at the edge of the garden to keep Adam and Eve from returning to their previous home (Genesis 3:24).

In the book of Ezekiel we find the key to the appearances of a Cherubim. Ezekiel 1:6 says each one of the 4 described had four faces and four wings. Their 4 faces included that of a man, a lion, an ox and an eagle (vs.10). Ezekiel 10:1 lets us know those creatures were Cherubim.

Cherubim on the veil separating the "Holy of Holies" from the "Holy Place" lets us know that access was denied unless it was specifically authorized by God Himself. Access occurred only once a year by the high priest with the blood offering.

When Jesus died on the cross the veil in the tabernacle was ripped from the top to the bottom at the very moment of his passing! It was at this point God had received the sacrifice he had desire from before the beginning of time. The sacrifice of bulls and goats is no longer effective for the Jews or anyone else. The veil represented Jesus' body and when he died the "Holy of Holies" was opened where the "Ark of the Covenant" would have been. Jesus' death broke down the barrier between the Jew and the Gentile as well (Ephesians 2:14). Since Jesus' death, burial, resurrection and the out pouring of the Holy Spirit at Pentecost there is now a way to enter into the presence of God. Jesus is the way into the throne room!

The "Ark of the Covenant" had 2 Cherubim on it as if to warn the high priest not to tamper, but to do what he was instructed to do in the "Mosaic Law". The high priest did not have access to the contents of the ark! Jesus Christ spiritually has gained access to the true provisions of God. The ark contained the 2 tablets Moses received from God, the golden pot with manna and Aaron's rod that budded. The contents of the ark must be understood spiritually to gain any sense of God's intentions.

The tablets represented covenant with God, the golden pot with manna represents provision and Aaron's rod that budded speaks of eternal life! The "New Covenant" works in the heart and not in stone or the letter of the law. Through Christ Jesus we have provision (Philippians 4:19) and the promise of eternal life (John 3:16 and Romans 6:22)!

The Mosaic Law was given to Moses by God at Mount Sinai after Israel had journeyed from Egypt. Almost everyone has seen the movie The Ten Commandments starring Charleton Heston. The movie and the book of Exodus tell us the story of Israel's release from bondage by Pharaoh. Few people have seen the spiritual application for us today. Israel's bondage in Egypt, freedom from Pharaoh and receiving of the law at Mount Sinai are all types and shadows of the new birth.

Pharaoh is a type of Satan who holds people in bondage through sin. Just as the children of Israel wanted to be free so does the human soul want to be free from the condemnation and guilt sin brings. God forced Pharaoh's hand through 10 different plagues. The last plague was the death of the first born throughout the land, both man and beast (Exodus 11:5). God instructed Moses that every household should pick a lamb without any defect or blemish, kill it at evening and apply the lamb's blood to the door post and lintel (Exodus 12:5-7). When God's judgment came upon Egypt the destroyer would bypass every house where the blood was applied. The children of Israel that obeyed were saved when judgment passed over them!

> Exodus 12:13 And the blood shall be to you for a token upon the houses where ye *are:* and when I see the blood, I will pass over you, and the plague shall not be upon you to destroy *you,* when I smite the land of Egypt.

It was no coincidence that Jesus died on the Jewish celebration of Passover. John the Baptist stated Jesus is the Lamb of God who would take away the sins of the world (John 1:29). It is faith in the blood sacrifice of Jesus Christ that is needed to secure forgiveness of sins. Apostle Peter said that Jesus' blood must be applied to our lives for forgiveness. Many have questioned Peter's authority in requiring the baptism in Jesus' name for the remission of sins. Jesus has given Peter all the authority required!

Matthew recorded that Jesus gave Peter the "keys to the kingdom" saying, "whatsoever thou shalt bind on earth shall be bound in heaven: and whatsoever thou shalt loose on earth shall be loosed in heaven (Matthew 16:19)." Apostle Peter preached the 1st sermon of the "New Covenant" piercing the hearts of men and women with the word of God. After those powerful words were spoken Peter was asked what they should do. Peter told them that they needed to repent and be baptized in Jesus' name and their sins would be forgiven (Acts 2:38).

Baptism in Jesus' name is the application of his blood. A person exercises their faith through obedience to God's word. James wrote that faith without works, or doing God's word (corresponding action), causes that person's faith to be dead (James 2:20-26)! We understand God's word says that a person is saved by grace through faith. It would be a rhetorical question to ask what would have been the result of a father not applying the blood of the lamb on the door frame of the house before God's judgment came through the land! We can see those Israeli families in Egypt were saved because of faith in God's word declared by Moses. The fathers' obedience in applying the blood brought salvation to the families inside! Apostle Paul explains that being water baptized is being buried with Jesus in his death (Romans 6:4 and Colossians 2:12). This action is the application of the blood of Jesus Christ to our lives! The Holy Spirit baptism is not being discussed in these scriptures as it is obvious you are not buried when you receive the Holy Spirit (Pure Life). You are receiving life from above when the Holy Spirit enters and a person becomes a new creation in Christ (2 Corinthians 5:17 and Galatians 6:15)!

After Pharaoh let God's people go free he changed his mind and sent his soldiers to bring the children of Israel back or kill them. Three days after being freed Israel found that they were trapped between Pharaoh's army and the Red Sea. God moved again by opening a dry path through the Red Sea, which allowed Israel to flee to safety on the other side (Exodus 14:27). In the attempt to follow Israel through the Red Sea Pharaoh's army drowned (vs. #28).

The blood of the lamb and passing through the sea brought about the deliverance of Israel freeing them from the grips of Pharaoh! The death of Jesus on the cross in association with baptism in his name, fully submerged, brings deliverance to one's soul and the forgiveness of sins. Apostle Paul says that the body of sin, the entire sin dilemma, is destroyed or abolished in the baptism in Jesus' name (Romans 6:6)!

Jesus died, was 3 days in the heart of the earth and then he was resurrected. Israel went 3 days from Pharaoh's control, went down through the Red Sea and onto the other side safe. It was 50 days after Israel went through the Red Sea they found themselves at Mt. Sinai where they received the word of God on stone tablets. It was 50 days after Jesus' resurrection that those in the upper room received the Holy Spirit in the fleshly tables of the heart (2 Corinthians 3:3)!

What shall we then say that all the Old Testament stories are just fables? Is there not enough evidence to convince the reader that Jesus Christ is the only way to God and not just a way? As stated in God's word, the Mosaic Law was a shadow or rough outline of good things to come in Christ Jesus. Apostle Paul said the law was for instruction to bring the Jews to Christ (Hebrews 10:1 and Galatians 3:24-25). I pray God's words continue to persuade others to believe in the Lord Jesus and find access to the throne room and presence of God!

Chapter 4

A BIBLICAL LOOK AT SALVATION

The Merriam-Webster Dictionary says that salvation is to be understood as: 1. *a*: deliverance from the power and effects of sin, *b*: the agent or means that effects salvation, 2. liberation from ignorance or illusion and 3. *a*: preservation from destruction or failure, and *b*: deliverance from danger or difficulty. Salvation of the believer encompasses all of these areas defined.

The apostle Paul wrote approximately one third of the New Testament and these words, "For I am not ashamed of the gospel of Christ: for it is the power of God unto *salvation* to every one that believeth; to the Jew first, and also to the Greek (Romans 1:16)". The New Testament word salvation from the Greek (Young's Concordance #G4991) means deliver, health, save and saving. The apostle John wrote, "For God sent not his Son into the world to condemn the world; but that the world through him might be saved (John 3:17)". The definition of the word saved from the Greek (#G4982) means to heal, preserve, save and be (make) whole. The words salvation and saved are not just "church lingo", but truly they are from the word of God. God's word lets us know that man has the need to be saved, delivered or rescued from something.

Is the bible the true word of God? To many people the bible is a literary work and to others it's just the writings of old men. To the church the bible is the God breathed, God inspired will of our Creator given to men for the purpose of redemption and salvation. The story of Adam and Eve is nothing more than a fairy tale to the skeptic. To the believer the "Adamic Curse" gives us understanding of the sin nature that we all have to overcome. The human race needs to be set free or saved from condemnation brought about by sin and the sin nature.

Luke 3:23-38 gives us the linage of Jesus all the way back to Adam. The Apostle Paul writes in 1 Corinthians 15:22 that in Adam all die. Romans 7:14 lets us know that all humanity is carnal, sold under sin. We understand then that in the family of Adam we all have a sin nature. Condemnation is upon each of us because of sin. The sin nature is therefore a curse because it initiates sin. Note that Romans 7:5 says, "For when we were in the flesh, the motions (G3804 – emotions, influence or affections) of sins, which were by the law, did work in our members to bring forth fruit unto death".

There is great good news for mankind and it is the gospel of Jesus Christ. The gospel of Jesus Christ is the power, strength and authority of God that brings us salvation. "<u>There is therefore now no condemnation to them which are in Christ Jesus, who walk</u> (live) not after the flesh, but <u>after the Spirit</u>. For the law of the Spirit of life in Christ Jesus hath made me free from the law of sin and death (Romans 8:1-2)".

Apostle Paul wrote to the church in Corinth (those already saved), "Moreover, brethren, I declare unto you the gospel which I preached unto you, which also ye have received, and wherein ye stand; By which also ye are saved, if ye keep in memory what I preached unto you, unless ye have believed in vain (1 Corinthians 15:1-2)". These biblical truths are elementary and the understanding of the sin nature is basic knowledge to the Christian faith. However, the way in which we are freed from sin and its hold upon our lives has fractured the unity of God loving people, causing denominational boundaries or barriers that the Christian community is afraid to take on or even examine.

In the life of a Christian it is necessary to know God's truths and not be swayed by man's opinion. We must therefore understand salvation from God's perspective through His word. God's word is His will and must be preeminent in our belief system. Faith comes through the understanding of God's word and not by the traditions of men. It is very clear that faith is generated out of knowing God's word to be true (Romans 10:17).

Apostle Paul posed a rhetorical question asking what if some do not believe, shall their unbelief make the faith of God without effect (Romans 3:3)? He answers the question in verse 4, "God forbid: yea, let God be true, but every man a liar; as it is written, That thou mightest be justified in thy sayings, and mightest overcome when thou art judged".

We must remember that when the Apostle Paul writes to the churches he is writing to those who were already freed from the condemnation brought about by sin. The King James refers to those he is writing to as saints. Saints are simply those who have been "sanctified" or set apart from sin. He reminds us in Ephesians 2:1 & 5 and Colossians 2:13 that the "saints" were dead in trespasses and sins but have been made alive together with Christ. Let us once again consider Paul's words: Romans 8:1-2, "There is therefore now no condemnation to them which are in Christ Jesus, who walk not after the flesh, but after the Spirit. For the law of the Spirit of life in Christ Jesus hath made me free from the law of sin and death,"

Salvation of mankind has come at the expense of the life of Jesus the anointed one, the Christ. We all need to understand that God is requiring that the atoning blood of His son, Jesus of Nazareth, be applied to our lives to be saved! The application of Jesus' blood to one's life is understood through scriptural integrity. When scripture is taken out of its proper context it becomes a pretext to support someone's philosophy. Unfortunately over time philosophy becomes tradition. Jesus said, Well did Isaiah prophesy of the hypocrites, as it was written, people honor me with the things they will confess, but their desires are not for me. Their worship of me has no benefit for them because they teach the commandments of men and not doctrinal truths ordained of God. They set aside God's mandates and hold to their traditions. They completely reject His commandments to keep their own traditions (my paraphrase of Mark 7:6-9).

Only God can save and salvation is through His son Jesus Christ alone. Jesus said that he was the way, the truth and the life. He declared no one has access to God the creator except through him (John 14:6).

Let's examine very familiar scriptures in "Christendom". The Apostle Paul wrote that if we will confess with our mouths the Lord Jesus, and if we will believe in our hearts that God hath raised Jesus from the dead we will be saved. With the heart man believes unto righteousness; and it is with the mouth our confession is made unto salvation. The scripture says that whosoever believes on Jesus will not be ashamed (Romans 10:9-11). These scriptures at face value may appear to be scripture to hang your salvation on. Let's look closer. First, scholarly consensus tells us that the book of Romans was written by the Apostle Paul to the church in Rome somewhere around 56 A.D. to 58 A.D. The church of Jesus Christ came into being on Pentecost, 50 days after Jesus' resurrection, when the Holy Spirit was given to those in the upper room in Jerusalem around 31 A.D. to 33 A.D. The upper room experience at Jerusalem was the very beginning of the church age. The book of Romans was probably written somewhere between 20 to 30 years after the church began. Scripture tells us that God made Jesus a life giving spirit (1 Corinthians 15:45) and that no one was born of the spirit until after Jesus was glorified, after his death, burial and resurrection (John 7:38).

Was the message of the apostle Peter at Pentecost precise? Did Peter have the authority from Christ to speak? Was Peter's message confirmed by other apostles? These are all rhetorical questions and would be answered in the affirmative if answered. We will consider that message later.

As we consider Romans 10:9-11 let's think through the progression we find in the book of Romans. Chapters 1-8 addresses the condition of fallen humanity; that there were none righteous in God's sight, that the law made no one perfect, that repentance was necessary, that water baptism by faith caused believers to be buried with Christ in his death (which broke the back of sin), that there is a war between our desire to follow God's will and our flesh and finally with the spirit of Christ working in us we are free from the law of sin and death. Agreed, this was a very short and incomplete synopsis. Chapter 12 then begins to examine the life of holiness. Between chapters 8 and 12 there is a break in the flow. It's a 3 chapter parenthetical insertion. Chapters 9-11 are a digression focused on Israel. The Apostle Paul being a Hebrew from the tribe of Benjamin was very concerned about his brethren and said, "I could wish that myself were accursed from Christ for my brethren, my kinsmen according to the flesh; Who are Israelites … (Romans 9:3-4)". In verse 27 of chapter 9 Apostle Paul quoted Isaiah writing that even though the children of Israel were as the sand of the sea, a remnant would be saved. Listen to the apostle's heart in verses 1-3, "I say the truth in Christ, I lie not, my conscience also bearing me witness in the Holy Ghost, That I have great heaviness and continual sorrow in my heart. For I could wish that myself were accursed from Christ for my brethren, my kinsmen according to the flesh".

Paul's mind was weighed down in grief for Israel's lack of faith at their rejection of the Messiah. This disquieting of the apostle's spirit sets the stage for Paul's account given in the 10th chapter. In Romans 10:1-4 Paul writes, "Brethren, my heart's desire and prayer to God for Israel is, that they might be saved. For I bear them record that they have a zeal of God, but not according to knowledge. For they being ignorant of God's righteousness, and going about to establish their own righteousness, have not submitted themselves unto the righteousness of God. For Christ *is* the end of the law for righteousness to every one that believeth."

Consider now what the apostle writes to the church at Rome, "But the righteousness which is of faith speaketh on this wise, Say not in thine heart, Who shall ascend into heaven? (that is, to bring Christ down *from above*:) Or, Who shall descend into the deep? (that is, to bring up Christ again from the dead.) But what saith it? The word is nigh thee, *even* in thy mouth, and in thy heart: that is, the word of faith, which we preach (Romans 10:6-8);" Paul explains right standing with God or righteousness is realized through faith in the words that the apostles had already shared with the church at Rome, the saints. The apostles continued to preach the same truths after the day of Pentecost. Words of faith are not just for the new birth, but words that if believed will protect and deliver us from our adversary as we move through life.

Romans 10:9-12 states, "if thou shalt confess with thy mouth the Lord Jesus, and shalt believe in thine heart that God hath raised him from the dead, thou shalt be saved. For with the heart man believeth unto righteousness; and with the mouth confession is made unto salvation. For the scripture saith, Whosoever believeth on him shall not be ashamed. For there is no difference between the Jew and the Greek: for the same Lord over all is rich unto all that call upon him." In other words, if we will speak God's words of truth concerning Christ Jesus as declared by the apostles and know that they are true, we will see victory in our lives whether Jew or Gentile!

These words of faith were preached to the early saints by the apostles. First there are words that lead to new life in Christ and then there are other words that lead to victory through Christ Jesus. A child of God must believe the words concerning Jesus' life, death, burial, resurrection and his position of authority at God's right hand. Remember with the heart, mind and thought life a man believes God unto right standing or righteousness; and with the mouth confession, affirmation and declaration is made unto or until salvation, deliverance and victory comes. If we will declare with our mouths the apostolic words of victory in the Lord Jesus, and we are convinced in our minds that God hath raised Jesus from the dead to be our help, comforter and constant companion, through Jesus we shall be saved, delivered, protected and preserved. Jesus will never leave us or forsake us!

We should be able to see that Romans 10:9-11 is not a formula by which a person is born again even though it takes believing the words of the apostles to realize true salvation. The apostle Paul brings greater clarity in Romans 10:13-17 writing, "For whosoever shall call upon the name of the Lord shall be saved. How then shall they call on him in whom they have not believed? and how shall they believe in him of whom they have not heard? and how shall they hear without a preacher? And how shall they preach, except they be sent? as it is written, How beautiful are the feet of them that preach the gospel of peace, and bring glad tidings of good things! But they have not all obeyed the gospel. For Esaias saith, Lord, who hath believed our report? So then faith *cometh* by hearing, and hearing by the word of God."

There is truth to hear, a way to believe and a way to call. There also has to be a call of God through Christ Jesus to preach truth. The preacher must have God's word and people's souls in his or her heart. The true man or woman of God is compelled to speak God's truth, which will cause faith to rise within a person unto salvation. Paul wrote in 1 Corinthians 11:1-2, "Be ye followers of me, even as I also *am* of Christ. Now I praise you, brethren, that ye remember me in all things, and keep the ordinances, as I delivered *them* to you." Also in 1 Corinthians 15:1-2, "Moreover, brethren, I declare unto you the gospel which I preached unto you, which also ye have received, and wherein ye stand; By which also ye are saved, if ye keep in memory what I preached unto you, unless ye have believed in vain." These words are important for us to remember because it is vanity to believe the wrong thing even if your heart is right. How do we know this to be true?

Jesus made many alarming statements letting us know that not every one that calls on him will enter into the kingdom of heaven. He said we must do the will of God his Father. There will be those who will say to Jesus that they had prophesied in his name, in his name had cast out devils and in his name done many great works. But Jesus will say he never knew them and that they should go away because of their iniquity (Matthew 7:21-23).

No where in the words of the apostles or Jesus Christ is there ever an account of anyone telling potential believers just to say a sinner's prayer! No where! God's judgment is upon those who even unknowingly misrepresent, distort or otherwise change God's plan for man's salvation. The gospel in its true form is the strength by which we are saved. The church is built upon the foundation of the apostles not the traditions of men. We must therefore believe the words of truth penned by those called into service by Christ himself!

Galatians 1:8-12 But though we, or an angel from heaven, preach any other gospel unto you than that which we have preached unto you, let him be accursed. As we said before, so say I now again, If any *man* preach any other gospel unto you than that ye have received, let him be accursed. For do I now persuade men, or God? or do I seek to please men? for if I yet pleased men, I should not be the servant of Christ. But I certify you, brethren, that the gospel which was preached of me is not after man. For I neither received it of man, neither was I taught *it*, but by the revelation of Jesus Christ.

On the day of Pentecost and there after we hear the same words in the mouths of the apostles and other disciples, more than two or three witnesses. There is a way to know we are right with God and to know we are saved!

1 John 5:11-13 And this is the record, that God hath given to us eternal life, and this life is in his Son. He that hath the Son hath life; *and* he that hath not the Son of God hath not life. These things have I written unto you that believe on the name of the Son of God; that ye may know that ye have eternal life, and that ye may believe on the name of the Son of God.

John 3:16-18 (KJV) For God so loved the world, that he gave his only begotten Son, that whosoever believeth in him should not perish, but have everlasting life. For God sent not his Son into the world to condemn the world; but that the world through him might be saved. He that believeth on him is not condemned: but he that believeth not is condemned already, <u>because he hath not believed in the name of the only begotten Son of God</u>.

These scriptures tell us to believe in the name of Jesus. How do we then believe in his name? The Apostle Peter preached the first message at the beginning of the church age. Peter's message was true then and it is truth today. His words were given to him by revelation even as God revealed Jesus to him. Peter came to understand that the man he knew as Jesus of Nazareth was the Christ (Messiah), the son of the living God (read Matthew 16:15-19). The message of the "New Birth" and faith in the name of Jesus is found in Acts 2:38-39. It is a must read for everyone, even as many as the Lord our God shall call!

> Acts 2:38-39 Then Peter said unto them, Repent, and be baptized every one of you in the name of Jesus Christ for the remission of sins, and ye shall receive the gift of the Holy Ghost. For the promise is unto you, and to your children, and to all that are afar off, *even* as many as the Lord our God shall call.

Philip the evangelist preached the things concerning the kingdom of God, and the name of Jesus Christ. Those that heard his words were baptized, both men and women (Acts 8:12). The Apostle Peter preached Jesus to the first Gentiles who were saved and when they believed the words Peter spoke they were filled with the Holy Spirit. Peter commanded them to be baptized in the name of Jesus (Acts 10:45-48). The Apostle Paul arriving in Ephesus found disciples (G3101 pupils or people who are learning) and asked them if they had received the Holy Ghost since they believed what they were told about Jesus. They said they had not heard of the Holy Ghost. Paul then asked them how they were baptized. They told him by John's baptism. Paul instructed them how to believe on the name of Jesus Christ and they were baptized in the name of the Lord Jesus (Acts 19:1-5).

Apostle Paul gave his testimony concerning baptism in Acts 22:12-16, "And one Ananias, a devout man according to the law, having a good report of all the Jews which dwelt *there*, Came unto me, and stood, and said unto me, Brother Saul, receive thy sight. And the same hour I looked up upon him. And he said, The God of our fathers hath chosen thee, that thou shouldest know his will, and see that Just One (Jesus), and shouldest hear the voice of his mouth. For thou shalt be his witness unto all men of what thou hast seen and heard. And now why tarriest (delay) thou? arise, and be baptized, and wash away thy sins, calling on the name of the Lord."

Isaiah wrote asking the questions, who has believed their report and to whom has the arm of the Lord (Jesus) been revealed (Isaiah 53:1)? Salvation is in Jesus Christ and him alone. As the blood of the lamb at Passover was applied to the door posts and lintel by the command of God, so must the blood of Jesus be applied to our dwelling place according to God's word. The application of the blood of Jesus Christ is done through water baptism in Jesus' name! God said that when he saw the blood he would pass over and not bring judgment to that household. The family of God is no longer under condemnation for sin as they have had the blood of the spotless lamb, Jesus, applied to their temple. Our spiritual abode now having been cleansed is prepared for the life of Christ to dwell.

Many preachers say that baptism is not a saving ordinance, but what does the scripture say? They will argue that Mark 16:15-16 was not in the original transcripts but was added later. Well, God saw fit to have it there now! What other scriptures are they going to add or remove to satisfy their doctrine?

> Mark 16:15-16 And he said unto them, Go ye into all the world, and preach the gospel to every creature. <u>He that believeth and is baptized shall be saved</u>; but he that believeth not shall be damned. Take note that the gospel had to include baptism!

The Apostle Peter wrote that baptism does save us by the resurrection of Jesus Christ. He stated that it is not the putting away or washing away of the filth of the flesh, but the answer of a good conscience toward God (1 Peter 3:21). How does baptism in water make a difference? It is an answer of a good conscience, it is faith in action!

> Romans 6:3-6 Know ye not, that so many of us as were baptized into Jesus Christ were baptized into his death? <u>Therefore we are buried with him by baptism into death</u>: that like as Christ was raised up from the dead by the glory of the Father, even so we also should walk in newness of life. For if we have

been planted together in the likeness of his death, we shall be also *in the likeness* of *his* resurrection: Knowing this, that our <u>old man is crucified with *him*, that the body of sin might be destroyed</u>, that henceforth we should not serve sin.

In the New Testament book of James we read that a person's faith is dead or inoperative without corresponding action. James gives us an illustration by having us compare a body without the spirit to faith without doing what God has commanded i.e. works. If we say we have faith in God and Jesus and give no regard to doing what has been asked of us our faith is dead without doing (James 2:17,18, &26)!

This is where the heart of repentance is crucial! Repentance is death to self and our will. We realize that we must come into agreement with God and not just be compliant. When our hearts are to do God's will we will see what God's word demands for a covenant relationship. Baptism will apply the blood sacrifice of Jesus Christ when we are covered with water in Jesus' name. The indwelling of the Holy Spirit, or being born again from above, completes the new birth experience. The life of Christ known to be the Holy Spirit in this the "New Covenant" comes to abide in us and it brings miracle working power that helps us overcome temptation and the trials we all experience in this life.

> Colossians 1:26-27 … the mystery which hath been hid from ages and from generations, but now is made manifest to his saints: To whom God would make known what *is* the riches of the glory of this mystery among the Gentiles; which is <u>Christ in you, the hope of glory</u>:

> Colossians 3:4 When <u>Christ, *who is* our life</u>, shall appear, then shall ye also appear with him in glory.

> Galatians 2:20 I am crucified with Christ: nevertheless I live; yet not I, but <u>Christ liveth in me</u>: and the life which I now live in the flesh I live by the faith of the Son of God, who loved me, and gave himself for me.

Repented, baptized in Jesus' name, filled with the Holy Spirit and saved! What a wonderful testimony to have! But, there is so much controversy swirling around the core doctrinal teachings of the apostles. We must read, pray and ask the Lord for help when what we have been taught does not square with God's word. Critical thinking and examination of scripture is a must! We must approach what we have been taught from the position of cautious consideration. Holding a doctrinal view or interpretation at arm's length and examining it before accepting it into our belief system is a must.

> Isaiah 28:9-12 (KJV) Whom shall he teach knowledge? and whom shall he make to understand doctrine? *them that are* weaned from the milk, *and* drawn from the breasts. For precept *must be* upon precept, precept upon precept; line upon line, line upon line; here a little, *and* there a little: For with stammering lips and another tongue will he speak to this people. To whom he said, This *is* the rest *wherewith* ye may cause the weary to rest; and this *is* the refreshing: yet they would not hear.

Critical thinking is a mindset aimed toward discovering truth.

Chapter 5

JESUS CHRIST

How can the 2 centuries old controversy swirling around the doctrines defining who Jesus Christ is be brought to the light so that there is only truth which remains? The word of God is the answer! This solution may sound simplistic, but wait! The word of God tells us that all scripture is given by inspiration of God, and is profitable for doctrine, for reproof, for correction, for instruction in righteousness (2 Timothy 3:16). Scripture, the word of God, is valuable for knowing biblical truth! Search God's word!

When the Apostle Paul wrote his second letter to Timothy, his son in the faith (1Timothy 1:2), there was <u>no</u> bible with New Testament (NT) writings. The scriptures the apostle was referring to in 2 Timothy 3:16 had to be the Torah (Moses' 5 books) and the writings of the prophets. When we analyze the Old Testament (OT), we see many <u>prophecies</u> that should have helped the Jews recognize the Messiah.

There have been many debates over Psalms 110:1, <u>The LORD said unto my lord</u>, Sit thou at my right hand, until I make thine enemies thy footstool. It is such a waste of time and effort to keep disputing the definition of these two words (Lord and lord) when we have the entire OT and NT scriptures from which to draw our truth.

In Acts 17:1-2, we see the Apostle Paul going into the synagogue on the Sabbath and reasoning with the people out of the scriptures, OT. When Paul was a prisoner in Rome, he had many come to his quarters, and there Paul persuaded them concerning Jesus, both out of the Law of Moses, and out of the prophets (Acts 28:23). Following are a few references where OT scriptures prophesied of the Messiah, Jesus Christ. We must keep in mind that these scriptures are God breathed, and they are valuable for doctrine and teaching of the truth!

The very first scripture that speaks prophetically of the Messiah is found in Genesis 3:15 (authored by God and written by Moses): And I will put enmity between thee and <u>the woman</u>, and between thy seed and <u>her seed</u>; it shall bruise thy head, and thou shalt bruise <u>his</u> heel. Here we see the seed, or child, of the woman (child of human origin) will crush the head of the serpent. The prophesied Messiah will break the authority and control of Satan.

Moses also wrote the book of Deuteronomy. Jehovah, the God of Abraham, Isaac and Jacob who identifies Himself as the Lord our God (the Eternal, the supreme deity, i.e. the God of gods), told Moses that he would raise up unto Israel <u>a Prophet</u> <u>from the midst of them</u>, <u>of their brethren</u>, like Moses. Israel would be required to listen to this prophet and respond (Deuteronomy 18:15-18). This is another indication that the Messiah's DNA would be that of the family of Israel. We can verify that this prophecy concerns Jesus Christ by the NT (Acts 3:20-23).

The prophet Isaiah wrote many prophecies that show us who the Messiah would be as it relates to his humanity. In chapter 7:13-14, Isaiah writes to inform the <u>house of David</u> that God will give them <u>a sign</u>. The sign was that <u>a virgin</u> will become pregnant and give birth to <u>a son</u>. She would call his name Immanuel. The Jews were looking for a specific indication, a signal, to let them know God was still with them. At the time when a virgin would give birth to a male child without the natural means of procreation, the house of David (lineage from Judah) should be encouraged to know that God had not forsaken them! God provided a savior to redeem them, Jesus! In the NT we discover that this salvation is for the Gentile world also!

In chapter 9:6-7, Isaiah prophesied that a male child will be born unto Israel. The government would be upon his shoulder (his portion or responsibility). His name would be called Wonderful, Counselor, the mighty God, the everlasting

Father and the Prince of Peace. Isaiah wrote that of the greatness (H4766) of his government and peace there would be no border (H7093), and he would rule upon the throne of David. The NT tells us Jesus will rule the earth from Jerusalem for 1,000 years (Revelation 20:6)!

Isaiah chapter 11:1 says there shall come forth a rod (King David) out of the stem of Jesse, and a Branch (Jesus of Nazareth) shall grow out of his (David's) roots (pedigree). Jeremiah wrote, Behold, the days come, saith the LORD, that I will raise unto David a righteous Branch (Jesus), and a King shall reign and prosper, and shall execute judgment and justice in the earth (Jeremiah 23:5). Also Zechariah wrote, … Behold the man whose name is The BRANCH (Jesus); and he shall grow up out of his place, and he shall build the temple (the church) of the LORD (Zechariah 6:12). Again and again we have OT scripture proving who the Messiah would be.

Jesus, the anointed one of God, was born of a woman, and in the days of his earthly existence, he was subject to the Mosaic Law (Galatians 4:4). The OT scriptures make it very clear that Jesus was of the family of King David and will be seated on the throne (place of authority) once occupied by King David.

> Galatians 4:4-5 But when the fulness of the time was come, God sent forth (from Jordan) his Son, made of a woman, made under the law, To redeem them that were under the law, that we might receive the adoption of sons. (The parenthesis here is mine.)

As we continue to look at OT scriptures, let's go back to Isaiah chapter 11:2, which reads, "And the spirit of the LORD shall rest upon him, the spirit of wisdom and understanding, the spirit of counsel and might, the spirit of knowledge and of the fear of the LORD." God's word declares that the spirit (life) of the Lord (God the eternal) will rest upon the Messiah. Let's break these words down for better understanding. The word "spirit" is the Hebrew word rûach, (H7307-Young's), meaning breath or (figuratively) life! The word "Lord" is y^c hôvâh (H3068), meaning the one who abides by Himself alone, the eternal; Jehovah. Finally, the word "rest", nûach (H5117), means to dwell or remain. Simply stated, the life of God would dwell in Jesus, which would make Jesus the only begotten of the Father, full of grace and truth (John 1:14). The body of Christ receives the adoption of sons through Christ Jesus (Galatians 4:4-6)! Christ in us the hope of glory (Colossians 1:27)!

There is another scripture in the book of Isaiah that is similar to Isaiah 11:2. Isaiah 61:1 is a familiar verse, which is a prophecy of something the Messiah would and did say.

> Isaiah 61:1 The Spirit of the Lord GOD is upon me; because the LORD hath **anointed** me to preach good tidings unto the meek; he hath sent me to bind up the brokenhearted, to proclaim liberty to the captives, and the opening of the prison to them that are bound. *ANOINTED FOR MINISTRY!*

When we really consider what was said, Jesus told the leaders in the synagogue that the spirit, or life, of God was upon, or in, him. God had sanctified (set apart) Jesus for ministry, including the sacrifice of his life! This is not what is being widely taught in Christendom today, but it is the word of God!

We see in just these few OT scriptures that God purposed to bring forth the seed of a woman, who would be in the family of King David and who was destined to bring salvation to Israel. This human male was set apart (anointed or consecrated) for the purpose of telling forth God's word, blessing the people and offering himself as a sacrifice for sin! He will reign over the house of David from Jerusalem. There is nothing in the OT scriptures that would lead someone to believe Jesus was God. **Nothing!** During Jesus' lifetime here on earth, he taught his disciples and exhibited a life like no other man. The things Jesus said are essential to us! We must discern the impact they have for our lives!

Jesus asked his disciples, "who do men say **I the son of man am**"? Jesus promised that Peter would receive the keys to the kingdom of heaven *after* Peter identified Jesus, the son of man, as the Christ, son of the living God. Can one imagine being given the solutions for mankind's eternal wellbeing? **Peter was later given truths** (keys) **that would unlock the questions whereby we can become right with God and inherit eternal life (Matthew 16:13-19)**. That was authority given from Jesus for the "New Covenant". Peter understood the meaning of these things only after he received the Holy Spirit. The true church of Christ has those keys, should understand and should use them wisely!

If we get a good scriptural understanding of the Apostle Paul before his conversion, we know he hated Christians enough to arrest many and be complicit in the murder of others (Acts 7:58-59). Saul of Tarsus, whose name was later changed to Paul, had a great zeal for God and the Mosaic Law, but not according to God's "New Covenant" in Christ Jesus. Saul encountered Jesus while he was headed to Damascus to arrest Christians, and the direction for Saul's life was changed. Saul was taken to the home of a man named Judas, in Damascus. The 9th chapter of Acts will give the reader the whole story. Jesus told Ananias to go seek out Saul. Ananias was concerned about Saul coming to his house due to Saul's bad reputation. The response Jesus gave to Ananias is key here. Jesus told Ananias that <u>Saul was a chosen vessel and that he would bear Jesus' name before the Gentiles</u>, kings and the children of Israel (Acts 9:15-16). **Saul became the Apostle Paul upon his conversion**.

Jesus selected and affirmed these 2 men specifically, in scripture, giving them authority to speak on his behalf. The 17th chapter of John's gospel reveals Jesus' prayer to God concerning all the men God had given him for ministry. Jesus told God that he had given his disciples the words which God gave him. Jesus declares that his disciples received these words and that they knew that Jesus came out from God and was sent from God. In John 17:9 Jesus prayed, "I pray not for the world, but for them which thou hast given me; for they are thine". But that is not all he prayed! Verse #20 continues the prayer where <u>Jesus</u> says that <u>he prayed</u> not just for his disciples, but <u>for those also who will believe on him through their word</u>!! It is imperative that we believe on Jesus through the words of the apostles!

43

The first time we see the word "apostle" is in Romans 1:1 where Paul writes, "Paul, a servant of Jesus Christ, called to be an apostle, separated unto the gospel of God". The Greek word for apostle is apostolos (G652) and means "a delegate, specifically an ambassador, officially a commissioner of Christ, and he that is sent". We know the original apostles included both Peter and Paul. Before the Holy Spirit came in as a rushing mighty wind, the disciples in the upper room chose Matthias (Acts 1:26) as the replacement for Judas, but Jesus chose Paul. It would seem reasonable that a person claiming to be an apostle today would at least be declaring the "Apostles Doctrine" and not the traditions of men.

In that same chapter of Romans, the Apostle Paul makes it very clear who Jesus is when he writes concerning God's Son, **Jesus Christ our Lord**, which was "**made of the seed of David according to the flesh**" and "**declared to be the Son of God with power, according to the spirit of holiness**", by the resurrection from the dead (Romans 1:3-4). The word "according" in the Greek is kata (G2596), which means "touching or as pertaining to". Jesus is the offspring, or progeny, of David as pertaining to the flesh and the son of God as pertaining to the spirit (G4151-life) of holiness. Again, Jesus is the son of man according to the flesh, being born of a woman, and the son of God, having received the spirit or life from God at the river Jordan (Luke 3:22). In Luke 3:22, after Jesus receives the Holy Spirit (pure life), God declares of Jesus, "Thou art my beloved Son; in thee I am well please.

Apostle Paul wrote a letter to his son in the faith, Timothy, and told him to remember (keep in memory) that **Jesus Christ of** (G1537 or from) **the seed of David** was raised from the dead according to his gospel wherein he suffered trouble, as an evil doer … (2 Timothy 2:8-9).

Let's back up a bit to Acts chapter 2 where there is information that is overlooked too often. The Apostle Peter, who had been given the keys to the kingdom by Jesus, preached the first message of the "New Covenant". He gave us clarity regarding who Jesus was and how he was elevated to Lord and Christ by God. Peter declares that **Jesus of Nazareth was a man approved** (G584 accredited or set forth) **of God** among the Jews, through miracles and wonders and signs, which God did through Jesus. Peter did not say that *the Father* approved his son, but that *God* (G2316 the supreme Divinity or exceeding God) sanctioned or certified Jesus of Nazareth.

Peter also makes statements to Cornelius and his family that brings simplicity to the understanding of Jesus Christ. He shared that **God anointed Jesus of Nazareth** with the Holy Ghost and with power (sounds familiar): who went about doing good, and healing all that were oppressed of the devil; for **God was with him** (Acts 10:38). Peter did not say Jesus healed people because he was God!! Again, Peter did not say *the Father* or the *Spirit* anointed Jesus. It was *the creator* Himself, the bible says, who sanctified Jesus with the Holy Ghost (pure life). The bible tells us that Jesus was anointed with the oil of gladness (Holy Spirit) above his fellow man (Hebrews 1:9).

Isn't it interesting the way the Apostle Paul begins his letters to the churches? He will refer to Jehovah (the I Am) as the God and Father of the Lord Jesus Christ. Jesus worships the Creator who gave him life, authority and power. Matthew 28:18 makes it clear from the lips of Jesus himself that <u>all the power in heaven and earth was given to him</u>.

In the Apostle Paul's first letter to the church in Corinth, he lets us know that at the end of Jesus' 1,000 year reign he, will put down all rule and all authority and power and deliver up the kingdom to God (1 Corinthians 15:23-24). This truth being understood, Jesus will not hold onto the authority he was given. God will have accomplished His intended purposes for humanity! These verses draw a clear distinction between God and Jesus.

Jesus cannot be God the Creator if he intercedes for mankind. There is one mediator <u>between</u> God and the human race, the man Christ Jesus (1Timothy 2:5)! The word "mediator" is the Greek word mesitēs (G3316), which means "a go between or a reconciler". Think about a peanut butter sandwich! The peanut butter is flanked by 2 pieces of bread. The peanut butter is not a slice of bread, neither is Jesus God the Creator. Galatians 3:20 says a mediator is not a mediator of one, but *God is one.* The Apostle Paul lets us know that God is one side of the reconciliation and mankind is on the other side. The human race needs help to find peace with God. Jesus Christ is the "Great High Priest" who will present the church to God. Jesus Christ is our "Great Shepherd" protecting us for his master. Jesus is the "Vine" producing fruit through his branches for the farmer. Each example found in the NT lets us know that Jesus, the son of God, intercedes on our behalf and ministers between the Creator and ourselves! Jesus tells us that no one has access to God without coming to him first (John 14:6).

The writer of Hebrews, believed by many to be Paul, states that in this present age **God** is speaking to us through His son, whom **he/God** <u>appointed heir</u> of all things, by (G1722 because of or for the sake of) whom also **he/God** made the worlds (Hebrews 1:1-2). In these verses God is speaking, appointing, and has created all because of and for Jesus who is inheriting all things!

Many believe Jesus was involved in the creation. Again, how can you inherit something you made? Paul wrote the book of Colossians, and in that book, Paul writes a very similar verse. He writes for <u>by</u> (G1722 for the sake/benefit of) him (Jesus) were all things created, that are in heaven, and that are in earth, visible and invisible, whether they be thrones, or dominions, or principalities, or powers: all things were created <u>by</u> (G1223 because of) him, and for him (Colossians 1:16).

The writer of Hebrews and Paul, the writer of Colossians, penned that Jesus was the image of God (Hebrews 1:3 & Colossians 1:15). The word "image" is used in both scriptures, but really are different words in the Greek. In Colossians, the Greek word is eikōn (G1504 likeness, profile or representation) and in Hebrews, the Greek word is charaktēr (G5481 an exact copy or engraving). When you look in a mirror, do you see yourself? No, you see an image or reflection of your physical appearance. Jesus is a *reflection* of God's character spiritually because he always does those things that please God (John 8:29). When we examine Jesus' life, one can truly say they see love! Jesus operated out of the love of God that was manifest through the working of the Holy Spirit (pure life) that was dwelling in him. In the same way, the church is to be the image of Jesus Christ (Romans 8:29)!

The King James Bible tells us that faith comes by hearing, and hearing by the word of God (Romans 10:17). Faith comes through understanding the word of God. It is the preponderance of scripture (line upon line, precept upon precept/Isaiah 28:10-13) that brings clarity to the word of God. Isaiah 28:9 asks the question, "whom shall we teach knowledge and whom shall he make to understand doctrine?"

In the Synoptic Gospels, Jesus referred to himself as the son of man approximately 80 times. **John 13:31 Therefore, when he was gone out, Jesus said, Now is the Son of man glorified, and <u>God is glorified in him</u>.**

Chapter 6

CHRISTIANITY'S STRUGGLE WITH DECEPTION

Before Jesus was taken and crucified his disciples were with him on the Mount of Olives. They had several questions that were of concern to them. They asked Jesus when the temple buildings would be destroyed, what would be the sign of his return, and when would this age end. Jesus' answer was not an expected response. He told them to be careful that they were not deceived. Jesus explained to his disciples that there would be many people coming in the future declaring things in his name saying they were anointed to bring God's word. Jesus spoke of troubling times ahead for mankind (Matthew 24 & Luke 21). It is apparent Jesus was warning us also!

Deception implies trickery or dishonesty. We must identify the one who is the originator of lies and deception! Jesus said it was the Devil who was the father of lies (John 8:44). The very first deception in the bible was that of Eve. The serpent told Eve she could eat of the tree of "The Knowledge of Good and Evil" without concern for any retribution. Remember, God had told the man, Adam, that he could eat of any tree in the Garden of Eden except that one tree, "The Knowledge of Good and Evil"! God had told him that the day he ate from that tree he would surely die (Genesis 2:17). They both ate fruit from the forbidden tree!

God's word states that a day with the Lord is as a thousand years and a thousand years is as a day. The day they ate from that tree they died spiritually from the presence of God. Adam lived to be 930 years old and died. (Genesis 5:5) God keeps His word!

For a thousand years in thy sight *are but* as yesterday when it is past, and *as* a watch in the night. (Psalms 90:4)

But, beloved, be not ignorant of this one thing, that one day *is* with the Lord as a thousand years, and a thousand years as one day. (2Peter 3:8)

The Apostle Paul wrote approximately one third of the New Testament and by Jesus' own words Paul was to be an apostle to the Gentile nations of the world (Acts 9:15). Paul writes to the churches warning the saints and telling them not to be deceived.

Be not deceived; God is not mocked: for whatsoever a man soweth, that shall he also reap. For he that soweth to his flesh shall of the flesh reap corruption; but he that soweth to the Spirit shall of the Spirit reap life everlasting. (Galatians 6:7-8)

But evil men and seducers shall wax worse and worse, deceiving, and being deceived. (2Timothy 3:13)

Now I praise you, brethren, that ye remember me in all things, and keep the ordinances, as I delivered *them* to you. (1Corinthians 11:2)

Moreover, brethren, I declare unto you the gospel which I preached unto you, which also ye have received, and wherein ye stand; By which also ye are saved, if ye keep in memory what I preached unto you, unless ye have believed in vain. (1Corintnians 15:1-2)

It wasn't the Apostle Paul's intent to question the heart of those that would be believers in God. He was just warning of the error that would develop during the church age by those that were deceivers and by those that had been deceived.

In the 13th chapter of Matthew's Gospel Jesus speaks of the Devil's attempt to steal and destroy God's seed, His word. In verse 19 we see that when anyone hears the word of the kingdom and doesn't understand it the Devil will come and steal that word which was sown in their heart. This is the seed that has been sown by the wayside. In the 28th verse the enemy sows bad seed or tares in the field. Tares do not produce a harvest. In this verse the heart of man is the field that receives bad seed and there is no reproduction to reap. In this parable it is not God's truth that was being sown. False doctrine causes eternal death to those who believe the error.

In the 13th chapter of Matthew let me restate that Jesus is revealing the Devil's attempt to steal and destroy God's seed. The 33rd verse is very interesting in that Jesus says that the kingdom of heaven is like unto leaven, which a woman hid in three measures of meal, until the whole was leavened. The woman here, many agree, would represent a church. Leaven or yeast as we know produces fermentation (the breakdown of carbohydrates by microorganisms). The action of fermentation will ultimately cause whatever it is a part of to rot or become putrefied. The Apostle Paul wrote that a little leaven leavens the whole lump (Galatians 5:9). In other words, when leaven or yeast is mixed into a batch of dough the entire batch will rise or become changed. If left too long the batch will spoil!

Jesus said to beware of the leaven of the Pharisees (Matthew 16:6). These scriptures help us to understand the context of the leaven, which has been placed into three measures of meal. This was not a good thing. Meal is produced when seed becomes grain, which is then ground to make meal. The three measures of meal we can see are 3 separate groups. Each people group is united by the word they received, believed and teach. Remember the woman, a church, has added leaven or false doctrine into the mix. The error has now caused a very serious problem within these three groups. False doctrine has completely corrupted all three groups. In Ephesus the Apostle Paul called the elders of the church together and warned them that after his death grievous wolves would appear and they would not spare the flock (Acts 20:29).

Christendom has been corrupted by those seeking their own fame and fortune. The development of the Roman Church and its doctrines has corrupted the hearts and minds of men and women for over fifteen hundred years.

The Roman Church split and the Orthodox Catholic churches in the east were formed. Then out of the Reformation and over time the Protestant churches became prominent in the west. The same basic doctrines are in all three, which enables them to be unified in saying Jesus is God! This is not the instruction we receive from the Old or New Testaments. This is not the doctrine of the apostles and it is not what Jesus taught!

We understand from history that the apostle Paul was beheaded and the apostle Peter was crucified upside down for preaching the gospel in the name of Jesus. By the end of the first century all of the apostles had been martyred or died. It wasn't long that deception began to grow in the Gentile nations.

The Apostle John wrote the Gospel of St. John, 3 epistles or letters and the book of Revelation. In Revelation John quoted Jesus regarding the Nicolaitans. Jesus gave credit to the Ephesian church stating that "thou hatest the deeds of the Nicolaitans, which I also hate (Revelation 2:6)." The word Nicolaitan is interpreted to mean "conquer the laity." The Nicolaitans believed that a priestly order was needed to control the lay people.

In Acts 20:17 we see that Paul had gone to Ephesus and there called the elders of the church together. In that chapter Paul warns the church to beware of grievous wolves.

> Take heed therefore unto yourselves, and to all the flock, over the which the Holy Ghost hath made you overseers, to feed the church of God, which he hath purchased with his own blood (refers to Jesus vs. #24). For I know this, that after my departing shall grievous wolves enter in among you, not sparing the flock. (Act 20:28-29)

51

Terence Blackett noted the following in his writing, "Early Church History", posted May 9, 2010 by Barbados Underground:

> "The Nicolaitans arrogantly styled themselves Gnostics; that they were superior to Peter and Paul or any of Christ's other disciples, they alone had drunk of the supreme knowledge, are above principalities and powers, secure of their salvation and for that very reason they claimed that they were free to debauch women or indulge in all manner of licentiousness. They further claimed that this knowledge is of itself perfect redemption and sufficient. They lobbied for an ecclesiastical hierarchy to control the spiritual training of the laity. In other words, if the word of God could be taken away from the laity, the priesthood would have total control over its interpretation thus leading the congregation into the same lifestyle of the pagan religions."

After the apostles had gone off the scene bishops took control over Christians in the larger cities. Increasingly a hierarchy of clergy developed causing disputes regarding the titles and the roles of church leaders. This caused divisions within the church world. These disputes included the responsibilities of bishops and other church leaders. Even the words used to describe the office or position of church leadership was in debate.

One hundred years after the apostles were passed away the Roman Empire had hundreds of bishops throughout the civilized world of the Mediterranean and there were considerable disagreements in their doctrines. Around 200 A.D. Praxeas, a priest from Asia Minor, taught that the Father, the Son, and the Holy Spirit are just forms of the single person who is God. The Father, Son, and Holy Spirit are uninterrupted modes of one person.

Tertullian, a proponent of the Trinity, opposed Praxeas in his *treatise Adversus Praxean (against Praxeas - c.* 213). The precise term for Praxeas' teaching is **Modal Monarchianism**. Praxeas' doctrine can be found today in the Oneness

Pentecostal assemblies of the United Pentecostal (UPC) and United Apostolic Churches (UAC).

Paul of Samosata a Patriarch of Antioch concluded that Jesus Christ was a created being. The followers of Paul of Samosata believed that the followers of the Patriarch Alexander, a **Trinitarian**, were blaspheming, by elevating Christ to Godhood, when He was not divine. On the other hand, the Alexandrians were persuaded that the followers of Paul were blaspheming, by denying the divinity of Jesus Christ. **Dynamic Monarchianism** is the doctrine that Jesus Christ was a man conceived by the miracle working power of God and that Jesus was the Son of God having been filled with God's divine wisdom and power.

The doctrine known as Arianism actually began early in the 3rd century by Arius and was a further development of teachings of Paul of Samosata. Arius denounced the doctrine of the Alexandrian Christians and their concept of the Trinity, which almost caused war one with the other.

So in the early days of Christendom, but long after the apostles had left the scene we find three major Christian teachings concerning Jesus Christ. These three doctrines are **Modal Monarchiansim** (the Father, Son, and Holy Spirit are uninterrupted modes of one person, God), **Dynamic Monarchianism** (God is the Father, Jesus is a man and the Holy Spirit is a force or presence of God the Father) and the **Trinity** (the Father, Jesus and the Holy Spirit are the three persons of Godhead).

When Constantine won the battle of Milvan Bridge and finally became emperor of the Roman Empire he made Christianity the religion of the empire. Due to the turmoil brought about by the question of the person of Christ Constantine called for a council of bishops. At the Council of Nicaea Arius spoke persuasively in support of his doctrine. Athanasius, another Alexandrian, argued against the Arius' Doctrine, in favor of the absolute divinity of Christ. The majority of bishops at Nicaea condemned Arius' beliefs and excommunicated him. It is important to note here that they did not adopt the "Trinity" doctrine at that time. The philosophy of the Trinity was fashioned over the next couple of decades.

The bishops at the Council of Nicaea did by majority agree that the Father and the son, Jesus, were of the same substance. What was agreed upon led to the later Trinity doctrine.

Constantine was enraged that the Council of Nicaea had not unified his kingdom. Instead the Roman Empire became more divided. Arianism dominated for many decades even within the family of the Emperor. Constantine was not baptized until he was near death and that by an Arian priest.

Who then was and is deceived? These three doctrines prevailed in the Old World during the early centuries of Christianity. With three strong opinions and the controversies they have produced what must a person believe? Remember, Jesus said that we should not allow ourselves to be deceived. In the struggle for truth the Trinitarian Doctrine seems to have triumphed. But after all this confusion, disagreement and speculation shouldn't we really question whether or not the Trinity doctrine is God's truth? If we are to make our calling and election sure and if we are to work out our salvation with fear and trembling as the bible directs, should we just accept any premise without extensive examination of the word of God (2 Peter 1:10 and Philippians 2:12)?

It should be noted here that "Exegetes (those who interpret texts) and theologians today are in agreement that the Hebrew Bible does not contain a doctrine of the Trinity ... Although the Hebrew Bible depicts God as the Father of Israel and employs personifications of God such as Word, Spirit, Wisdom, and Presence, it would go beyond the intention and the spirit of the Old Testament to correlate these notions with later Trinitarian doctrine…" -- In the New Testament there is no reflective consciousness of the metaphysical nature of God ("immanent trinity"), nor does the New Testament contain the technical language of the later doctrine. Some theologians have concluded that all postbiblical Trinitarian doctrine is therefore arbitrary. It is incontestable that the doctrine cannot be established by scriptural evidence alone [The Encyclopedia of Religion, 1987]."

The many encyclopedias we have had access to for years have had in their pages information showing how the Catholic Church has changed truth into error. Error has over time become tradition. Please review these few examples:

Britannica Encyclopedia, 11th Edition, Volume 3, page 365 – <u>Baptism was changed</u> from the name of Jesus to words Father, Son & Holy Ghost in 2nd Century.

Canney Encyclopedia of Religion, page 53 – The early church baptized in the name of the Lord Jesus until the second century.

Hastings Encyclopedia of Religion, Volume 2 – Christian baptism was administered using the words, "in the name of Jesus." page 377. <u>Baptism was always in the name of Jesus until time of Justin Martyr</u>, page 389.

Catholic Encyclopedia, Volume 2, page 263 – Here the authors acknowledged that <u>the baptismal formula was changed by their church</u>.

Schaff – Herzog Religious Encyclopedia, Volume 1, page 435 – The New Testament knows only the baptism in the name of Jesus.

Hastings Dictionary of Bible, page 88 – It must be acknowledged that the three fold name of Matthew 28:19 does not appear to have been used by the primitive church, but rather in the name of Jesus, Jesus Christ or Lord Jesus.

Jesus said that we should believe on him through the words of the men God gave him, the apostles (John 17:20). No scripture of the bible can be or should be interpreted with one's own belief system influencing their understanding (2 Peter 1:20). The Apostle Paul wrote that we should keep in memory those truths he preached whereby we are saved (1 Corinthians 15:2).

Luke 1:35 And the angel answered and said unto her, The Holy Ghost (pure life) shall come upon thee, and the power (miracle working ability) of the Highest (God Himself) shall overshadow (invest supernatural influence upon) thee: therefore also that holy thing (man child-Luke 2:23) which shall be born of thee shall be (future) called the Son of God.

Roman 1:1-4 Paul, a servant of Jesus Christ, called *to be* an apostle, separated unto the gospel of God, (Which he had promised afore by his prophets in the holy scriptures,) Concerning his Son Jesus Christ our Lord, which was made of the seed of David according to the flesh; And declared *to be* the Son of God with power, according to the spirit of holiness, by the resurrection from the dead:

2Timothy 2:8-9 Remember that Jesus Christ of the seed of David was raised from the dead according to my gospel: Wherein I suffer trouble, as an evil doer, *even* unto bonds; but the word of God is not bound.

Truth is to be reasoned and believed. We all need to study God's word because ultimately it will be God himself that approves and saves us through His son!

Information has been gathered from many sources including: The Bible, Terence Blackett (Posted on May 9, 2010 by Barbados Underground), Wikipedia (an overview of early Christian history, see Early history of Christianity), carm.org, Encyclopedia Britannica Online and The Encyclopedia of Religion, 1987

Chapter 7

CRITICAL THINKING OR JUST CRITICAL

Many believers in Christ Jesus have been referred to as heretics and even the Apostle Paul was considered to be heretical by spiritual leadership of his day. In Acts 24:14 the apostle is quoted as saying, "But this I confess unto thee, that after the way which they call heresy, so worship I the God of my fathers, believing all things which are written in the law and in the prophets." In Paul's statement before the governor he declares that he believed all that was written by Moses and the prophets (Acts 28:17&23), which is now found in the "The Old Testament".

The dictionary states that a heretic is a dissenter from established religious dogma or one who dissents from an accepted belief or doctrine. The question that everyone should consider should be whether or not the accepted tenets of Christendom practiced by the majority are factually accurate with the bible.

A paradigm shift that would influence and profoundly transform the whole world had just taken place in the days of the apostles. The Jews did not understand this new movement and religious authority in that day fought against the fledgling church.

The beliefs of the early Christians were called heretical because their doctrine or teachings were a departure from the accepted beliefs and standards of Judaism in that day. Yes, the ritualistic practices of the Mosaic Law had been nullified. God was now doing a new thing through Jesus Christ's death, burial and resurrection.

New converts to Christianity were preaching faith by Jesus Christ and salvation through grace. This was not the accepted norm and spiritual leadership of that day persecuted the Christians even unto death. The first Christian martyr was Stephen who was stoned to death. As Stephen fell to his death he saw heaven open and Jesus Christ standing on the right hand of God (Acts 7:56-60).

Salvation of our souls is strictly our own responsibility. The bible lets us know that neither our parents, a spouse, a priest, not even a pastor can pray us into heaven or stand in our defense before God. Pastors will give an account before God concerning their flock, but we will stand alone giving explanation for the life we lived. Working out our salvation is something we need to do with the fear of God (Philippians 2:12).

Everyone who confesses that they believe in Jesus Christ should know for themselves, without question or hesitation, whether or not what they are taught is biblically accurate. Our eternal existence depends on it!

> 2 Timothy 2:15 Study to shew thyself approved unto God, a workman that needeth not to be ashamed, rightly dividing the word of truth.

> 1Timothy 4:16 Take heed unto thyself, and unto the doctrine; continue in them: for in doing this thou shalt both save thyself, and them that hear thee.

In most metropolitan area phone books we find listings for hundreds of Protestant denominations and sub groups. The Catholic Church is also divided up with many different orders or sects. The reason why there are so many divisions within "Christendom" is because there are so many differences in opinions and doctrinal teachings. Most mainline denominations attempt to unify by saying that they can fellowship because they all believe that Jesus died for their sins. The belief in the Trinity and "the sinner's prayer" are the principal doctrines of faith that make these groups feel that they are one, united in love.

Typically, they will say that when a person confesses Jesus with their mouth and believes in their heart that God raised him from the dead that person is saved. This belief is based on Romans 10:9 & 10. If you do not believe these core tenets or principles today then you are considered a heretic by mainstream Christendom! There is no question that the greater majority of professing Christians believe in a triune god and confession for salvation.

Are we more assured of eternal life following traditions of the majority or believing the unadulterated word of God? We should agree that the will of God revealed to us through the written words of His prophets and apostles carry His truth for mankind and not the considered opinion of many. Jesus made it very clear that the way to eternal life was a very narrow path for us all to travel. It requires faithfulness to God's word! Unfortunately, Jesus declared few would believe and find eternal life.

> Matthew 7:13-14 Enter ye in at the strait gate: for wide *is* the gate, and broad *is* the way, that leadeth to destruction, and many there be which go in thereat: Because strait *is* the gate, and narrow *is* the way, which leadeth unto life, and few there be that find it.

Apostle Paul taught the Jews truths concerning the Messiah out of the law and the prophets for at that time there was no New Testament. Paul used what are now "Old Testament" scriptures to point the Jews to Jesus Christ. He told them that the Mosaic Law was like a teacher to bring understanding concerning their Messiah. It was only a rough image or an outline of what God was doing in the New Covenant through Christ Jesus (Galatians 3:24-25 and Hebrews 10:1). These truths that Paul taught were in agreement with the other apostles; however Paul goes into a greater explanation of many truths in the epistles he wrote.

In 1 Corinthians 15:28 Paul writes that one day the son, Jesus, will be subject unto God who gave him all authority in Matthew 28:19. This scripture lets us understand that there is a difference in the ultimate authority over God's creation.

It is believed by many that the Apostle Paul also wrote the book of Hebrews. In Hebrews 1:2 we see that Jesus was appointed heir of all things, which would make one question how you could inherit something you were said to have created! Yes, we read in the King James Bible that the worlds were made by Jesus. One must understand that the word "by" comes from the Greek word dia', which is used as a preposition and can mean through, because of or even from. God made the worlds because of Jesus! Hebrews 1:10 tells us that God laid the foundations of the earth and the heavens are the works of His hands. Verse 13 confirms that it was Jehovah Himself who is the creator.

Based on just these 2 scriptures alone it is clear that God and Jesus are not the same person or even equal in their authority! Nowhere in the bible is there a record of Jesus professing that he was Jehovah the creator! Only where there is misunderstanding of scripture could one accept the idea that Jesus, the anointed one, is God. Jesus never claimed to be God!

John the Baptist told his followers that Jesus, the Christ (anointed) of God, would baptize them with the Holy Ghost and fire (Matthew 3:11). The Holy Spirit can also be understood to mean "Pure Life" (G40: pure, sacred - G4151: breath, mind or life)! New Testament scriptures are very clear that the Holy Spirit is the life of Jesus in us as a divine influence originating from God Himself. God made Jesus a life giving spirit (1 Corinthians 15:45) and now we can experience Christ in us the hope of glory (Colossians 1:27). Apostle Paul also refers to Christ as our life in his letter to the church in Colosse (Colossians 3:4).

The Apostle John brings clarity to the church's relationship with God and Jesus in his writings. We need to pay close attention to the words Jesus prayed to his Father in heaven. In John chapter 17 we read these words of Jesus, "Neither pray I for these alone (his disciples), but for them also which shall believe on me through their word; That they all may be one; as thou, Father, art in me, and I in thee, that they also may be one in us: that the world may believe that thou hast sent me. And the glory which thou gavest me I have given them; that they may be one, even as we are one: (John 17:20-21)". Now we can see what Jesus meant when he said I and the Father are one!

When Jesus said that he and the Father are one, he was not saying that he was God the Creator. Jesus did not mean to imply that he was the 2nd person of a Trinitarian godhead. Notice that <u>Jesus wants people to be one with God and himself</u>. He was referring to the unity of the spirit. God Jehovah's life was imparted to Jesus of Nazareth at the river Jordan when the Holy Spirit descended upon him. It was at that point God said, "this is my beloved son, in whom I am well pleased" (Matthew 3:17).

When a person receives the Holy Spirit it is "Pure Life" from Jesus Christ!

The Shema is the title of a prayer that serves as a centerpiece of the morning and evening Jewish prayer services and is found in Deuteronomy 6:4, "Hear, O Israel: the LORD is our God, the LORD is one". Jesus himself reaffirmed the truth in Mark 12:29 when he said, "… Hear, O Israel; The Lord our God is one Lord. The definition of the word one may be found in a Strong's Concordance number G1520, which means one or only.

The prophet Isaiah recorded a declaration made by God in chapter 45, verse 5. The Eternal stated, "I *am* the LORD, and *there is* none else, *there is* no God beside (H2108: except or save) me: I girded thee, though thou hast not known me". This same prophet also recorded another interesting prophecy, which foretold of the Messiah (Isaiah 61:1). Jesus actually read the very scripture!

Upon returning to Nazareth from the wilderness of temptation Jesus went into the synagogue on the Sabbath day and read from the book of Isaiah. He read the words that the Jewish leaders and priests knew without question. Jesus read, "The Spirit of the Lord *is* upon me, because he hath anointed me to preach the gospel to the poor; he hath sent me to heal the brokenhearted, to preach deliverance to the captives, and recovering of sight to the blind, to set at liberty them that are bruised, To preach the acceptable year of the Lord." Then he said, "This day is this scripture fulfilled in your ears (Luke 4:18-19 and 21)".

What is missed by so many is that Jesus was not only letting the Jews know that he was the Messiah, but Jesus was saying that he had received life from God Himself. This truth is hard for people to receive because of tradition. The Greek word (G4151) pneuma in Luke 4:18 and the Hebrew word (H7307) ruach in Isaiah 61:1 mean the same; spirit, wind, breath or life!

Jesus never claimed that he himself was Jehovah the eternal, Almighty God. A son is not his father! Reason tells us that a son obtains life from his father! This misunderstanding that Jesus is God comes from misinterpretation of scriptures formulated after the apostles had died. A son does not hold the same title as his parent.

The period from 100 A.D. through 325 A.D. began the questioning and suppositions as to who Jesus really was without regard to the simple truths shared by the apostles. The development and power of the Roman church sealed this error concerning who Jesus was, as well as so many other profane doctrines. Jesus made it very clear that he was the son of man and the son of God.

God's word says that Jesus was made the seed of David according to the flesh and declared to be the son of God by the spirit of holiness, by the resurrection from the dead (Romans 1:3-4). Jesus is the express image of God (Hebrews 1:3) and that is through the life he led in the spirit, a life of holiness: goodness, righteousness and truth. In the face of these previously mentioned scriptures concerning Jehovah God and His son Jesus the Christ (the anointed one), why is it that people are considered heretics when they believe them to be true.

The Old Testament word for Lord in Isaiah 45:3 is the word translated Jehovah (H3068-self-existing or eternal), which is found in the Young's concordance. To state that God by Himself is eternal and that He existed without the need for a 2nd or 3rd personality is not error. When the spirit of God moved upon the face of the waters it was the Lord God Himself, the omnipotent, speaking. There was no 3rd persona calling the worlds into existence as some have believed. Psalms 33:6 states that, "By the word of the LORD (H3068-the eternal) were <u>the heavens made; and all the host of them by the breath of **His** mouth</u>." Note that the pronoun is singular where it states it was the Lord's breath.

What then should we say about Jesus? Most professing Christians would say that they believe that Jesus was born of a woman. However, if we say that his flesh was the same as any man many people will start to withdraw themselves from us. Some would say Jesus couldn't have performed the miracles he did unless he was God. They will tell you that Jesus did not really have a human nature and his flesh wasn't like ours. Still, the bible we read, and say we believe, tells us there is one kind of flesh of men, I Corinthians 15:39. Where is the scripture that teaches us that Jesus' flesh wasn't like ours? How could Jesus of Nazareth be the lion of the tribe of Judah, the seed of Abraham or the seed of David if his DNA did not contain the human code of life from that family lineage? Deduction, supposition and sensual reasoning are futile when the word of God is so explicit.

How then did Jesus accomplish the miracles the disciples and apostles witnessed and wrote about? How was he able to heal if he wasn't God Himself? The answers are in the bible! Acts 2:22 states that Jesus was a man approved of God by the miracles that God did through him. Acts 10:38 states that Jesus went about doing good and healing all that were oppressed of the Devil because God was with him.

Take notice as to what these scriptures do say, but also what they don't say! Acts 2:22 & Acts 10:38 together tell us that Jesus, a Nazarite Jew, was a man approved, set forth or certified by God through the miracles, which God Himself did through Jesus. Because of the anointing, consecration or blessing of God that was upon him and the fact that God was with Jesus, Jesus was able heal all that were afflicted of the Devil! The 2 scriptures referred to in Acts spoke of God (G2316"Theos"-the supreme divinity) being with Jesus but it did not say the "Father" was with him. The scripture did not say the Triune God was with him either.

If Jesus is the 2nd person of the Trinity wouldn't it be more accurate to say the Father and/or the Spirit was with him? The writers of the various books of the bible wrote under the inspiration of God and their words mean what God intended! It is a shame that when a person declares that they believe Jesus was first the son of man and then was declared to be the son of God as stated in Romans 1:3-4 they labeled a heretic.

The virgin birth is an enigma with many people today. They will say things like, "God wrapped Himself in flesh and became a baby in Mary's womb". Why would our creator do that? Neither does the word of God say Jesus had God's spirit when he was born and in the manger. Again, the study of scripture brings enlightenment.

The word Mary received was that she was going to have a son without the baby being conceived the natural way. Most professing Christians do understand and believe it wasn't Mary lying with Joseph or some other man that caused her pregnancy. The conception of Jesus was not the sperm from a man but the power of Almighty God Himself! Remember, Jesus was made of a woman (Galatians 4:4) Look at what the angel told Mary:

> Luke 1:30-35 And the angel said unto her, Fear not, Mary: for thou hast found favour with God. And, behold, thou shalt conceive in thy womb, and bring forth a son, and shalt call his name JESUS. He shall be great, and shall be called the Son of the Highest: and the Lord God shall give unto him the throne of his father David: And he shall reign over the house of Jacob for ever; and of his kingdom there shall be no end. Then said Mary unto the angel, How shall this be, seeing I know not a man? And the angel answered and said unto her, The Holy Ghost shall come upon thee, and the power of the Highest shall overshadow thee: therefore also that holy thing which shall be born of thee shall be called the Son of God.

We just read that the Holy Ghost (pure life) would come upon Mary, the power (G1411 miraculous ability and strength) of the Highest (G5310/hupsistos-most high or supreme God) would overshadow (G1982-episkiazo, cast a shade upon, envelope or figuratively to *invest*-with PRETERNATURAL influence) her. Pay close attention to the word preternatural, which means: 1: existing outside of nature 2: exceeding what is natural or regular 3 : inexplicable by ordinary means.

The word preternatural is the key to understanding how Mary became pregnant with Jesus. The miraculous power and strength of God Himself invested within Mary that which is outside of the natural order. Just as God's breath moved upon the face of the waters when he spoke, just as God blew into man the breath of life, God by Himself spoke life into the womb of a virgin girl. God invested in or endowed Mary with something that had never been before and the virgin conceived. The scripture proclaims with loud scriptural certainty that Jesus was born through the power of God and not a miraculous entry of God Almighty into His creation. By the word of God this is truth!

> Galatians 4:4-5 But when the fulness of the time was come, God sent forth his Son, made {G1096 caused to be} of a woman, made under the law, (5) To redeem them that were under the law, that we might receive the adoption of sons.

Jesus will rule earth from his throne in Jerusalem for 1,000 years. Isaiah 9:7 tells us that the Prince of Peace will reign upon the throne of his father David, a former king of Israel. Why would God want to be seated upon an earthly throne? It makes no sense. Isaiah 66:1 says heaven is God's throne and the earth is His footstool, so the question must again be asked, what kind of house on earth could be built for God? The foregoing being understood, and common sense prevailing, why is it people are maligned for believing God's word?

Apostle Peter, the man of God, spoke truth in that great message he preached on the day of Pentecost following the death, burial and resurrection of Jesus Christ (Acts chapter 2). His words are as true now, 20 centuries later, and cannot be changed by man's tradition! God won't allow it! Peter was given the keys to the kingdom of heaven, truth that unlocks eternal life for those who will exercise faith in them (Matthew 16:19). People were moved by the word of God he preached and asked what they should do. Believe Peter's response by the Spirit:

> Act 2:36-38 Therefore let all the house of Israel know assuredly, that God hath made that same Jesus, whom ye have crucified, both Lord and Christ. Now when they heard *this*, they were pricked in their heart, and said unto Peter and to the rest of the apostles, Men *and* brethren, what shall we do? Then Peter said unto them, Repent, and be baptized every one of you in the name of Jesus Christ for the remission of sins, and ye shall receive the gift of the Holy Ghost.

Today when you share the need for repentance, baptism or even receiving the Holy Spirit there are those who will adamantly state you are in error because of Romans 10:9 & 10. The Apostle Paul, in the book of Romans, was writing to a Christian community, the church in Rome. He was not teaching on salvation to those already saved!

The progression through the book of Romans is a pathway to understanding what a person as a Christian should understand. The journey allows a saved person to grasp the truth about the sin nature, what real faith looks like, what was accomplished by water baptism, the struggle or fight with the sin nature and the blessing of having the Holy Spirit. That trip takes you from chapter 1 all the way through chapter 8. Chapters 9-11 are a diversion in the mind of the writer, a parenthetical insertion in the text. Now the apostle Paul focuses on Israel and expresses his concern. He could almost wish himself accursed for the sake of his brethren, Israel. They have rejected their Messiah! In chapter 10 the apostle states his desire that Israel would be saved. He is sharing his heart to the saints in Rome, Italy. He declares that Israel is ignorant when it comes to the will and righteousness of God.

Paul explains that for believers, Christ is the end of the law as far as right standing with God is concerned. When Jesus died on the cross the veil of the temple was ripped from the top to the bottom like an old cloth instead of a very thick curtain. God signified that He had done away with the Old Testament sacrifices and its rituals. Now the Jews, and all of Israel, must exercise faith in Jesus Christ for salvation! Paul wrote that the separation between the Jew and

Gentile has been done away with in Christ (Ephesians 2:14). The apostle knew that Israel and the Jews were without hope of eternal life if they did not believe in the Messiah.

Paul further informed the church in Rome that God's righteousness, which is through faith in Jesus Christ, they had already believed and experienced. God's word concerning Jesus was in their mouths (they were speaking it) and in their hearts (they believed it). It was the truth that the apostle had taught them, which worked not only for the new birth but for righteous living too. Paul had taught the churches that if they believed with their hearts the truths about Jesus (victory through his death, burial and resurrection) and confessed those truths they would be delivered or saved. For with the heart a man believes unto righteousness and with his mouth he confesses unto salvation (Romans 10:10)! Romans 10:9-10 was not what the apostles preached to the people for salvation. To find scripture for salvation we must return to the book of Acts where the church age began. We must examine carefully the messages given by the apostles and other ministers at the beginning. Salvation by faith in the word of God started with the Pentecostal experience (Acts chapter 2) and predated the letter to the Roman church by approximately 25-30 years.

Today, if you are able to share the truth with someone and he or she will really hear you, it is a wonderful thing. Most of Christendom is afraid to discuss the word of God and correctly apply scripture. An attempt to share God's word is rejected by most people as soon as the word of God is introduced. God's word must be understood and shared line upon line precept upon precept (Isaiah 28:9-10). Scriptures taken out of context become a pretext and many times a new denomination! Jesus made it clear when he said that traditions of men have made God's word ineffectual. He said in vain they do worship me (Matthew 15:9)!

Apostle Paul understood the pain of rejection by others when he tried to share Jesus Christ through the word of God. **Most people can't understand that it's not a matter of judging others, but a sincere desire to see them safe**

in Christ! The Apostle Paul wrote that all who live godly in Christ will suffer persecution (2 Timothy 3:12)! This is so true, nevertheless we persevere.

> 2 Timothy 2:8-10 Remember that Jesus Christ of the seed of David was raised from the dead according to my gospel: Wherein I suffer trouble, as an evil doer, *even* unto bonds; but the word of God is not bound. Therefore I endure all things for the elect's sakes, that they may also obtain the salvation which is in Christ Jesus with eternal glory.

Christians should share their faith demonstrating the confidence they have in the word of God. But it is wrong to critically judge another's views without thoroughly understanding their position or having done your own homework. To make the claim that someone is a heretic based on tradition is irresponsible and detrimental to those who would judge. We are instructed to study and show ourselves approved of God (2 Timothy 2:15). We should put forth the effort to know what the word of God is saying and then share. Belief in the traditions of men has destroyed the eternal hope of so many. Jesus said that it was futile or vain to worship God through the instructions, commandments and traditions of men (Mark 7:7-8).

Accusations brought about by well-meaning people have damaged many sincere believers in Christ. By trying to pull tares, much wheat has been damaged and some even destroyed. If you call a person a heretic, not fully understanding why they believe a certain way, you may have shattered their reputation and unwittingly assassinated them in the minds of others. Be careful not to injure God's precious people!

Critical thinking is a mindset aimed toward discovering truth.

Chapter 8

THE RAPTURE OF THE CHURCH

PRE-MID-POST

"The Rapture" is no small topic when it comes to biblical discussions! Many people believe that the idea Christians would someday be miraculously removed from earth to a heavenly home to be somewhat preposterous. I wonder what you think. I pray this information with help you make an educated decision regarding your position.

Fifty years ago there wasn't much known or taught concerning "the rapture of the church". It probably wasn't until Hal Lindsey wrote "The Late Great Planet Earth" that prophecy became much of an interest. Now more than a half century later bible prophecy is on the minds of most Christians as well as many others. The Y2K hype and the flawed Mayan end of the world scenario have cooled some of the enthusiasm. However, those who study God's word in any depth are still tuned in to the prophetic words for the last days.

The rapture is one subject that genders many differing opinions. Whether it is true or not I will let the reader decide for themselves. We realize that it doesn't matter what we think about any biblical issue. God's word is true, and if the rapture will occur, how we feel or what we believe will not prevent the fulfillment of His word!

There are 3 main views regarding the "rapture" and how it is related to the time of the "Great Tribulation". The "Pre-Trib Rapture" is the belief that the true church of Jesus Christ will be taken out of the earth before the tribulation period, which lasts for 7 years. In this view the church would not face or endure the effects God's judgment that comes upon planet earth. The proponents of the "Mid-Trib Rapture" believe the rapture of the church will occur half way through the tribulation. This would mean that the Christian Church would be on earth for 3½ of the 7 years of judgment. "Mid-Trib" philosophy presumes God would somehow keep the true believers safe during this period. Finally the "Post–Trib Rapture" advocates say the church will be on earth throughout the tribulation to be taken up at the end of this 7 year period and then returned right back to earth with Jesus when he comes back.

The "Post –Trib Rapture" view seems hard to accept if we are to believe that the true church has to experience the entire "Great Tribulation". In fact, the church really wouldn't go through the entire 7 years if they were caught up and then return with Jesus at the battle of Armageddon (Revelation 19:11-21).

Reading the book of Revelation and doing the math it is estimated that fully ½ of the earth's population will die or be killed during the 7 years of tribulation (Revelation 6:8 and 9:18). Why will God judge mankind with such devastating results? This must first be understood before we will ever understand the reason for a catching away of the church. Out of all the many ethnic groups, skin colors and cultures there are only 3 categories God is really dealing with; the Israelis (includes the Jews), Gentiles and the true church. All the families of the earth are Gentiles except for the family of Jacob also known as Israel. The 3rd group is the body of Christ, the true church, who are believers called out of the Israel and the Gentile nations.

God made a covenant with Abraham that brought a blessing to his offspring. These blessings and promises of God were passed down to Isaac, to Jacob (Israel) and then to his 12 sons. The Gentiles living at that time were without any relationship with God and considered reprobates or sinners. We can see this to be true in Apostle Paul's letter to the church in Ephesus. He reminds them that they had been Gentiles in the flesh and considered outsiders from the shared blessings of Israel (commonwealth). They previously had no covenant relationship, no hope, and they had lived without God and His blessings (Ephesians 2:11-12). Clearly stated, today, Jew or Gentile, if you do not have a relationship with God through the Lord Jesus Christ you have no claim to the blessings of God, and you are without hope (hopeless).

Israel committed great sin against God in direct disobedience to His mandates. Just reading "The 10 Commandments" we see that God had given Israel very clear instructions regarding their worship, but through disobedience their sins became many. God said that Israel was to have no other gods before Him, meaning they should not prefer anything above Him. They were instructed not to carve out or make any images after any creature and they were not to worship or serve them (Exodus 20:3-5)

Over time the children of Israel began to worship false gods defiling the land and committing spiritual adultery with stones and with trees, presumably carved to the likeness of some animal (2 Chronicles 24:18 and Jeremiah 3:9). 2 Kings summarizes Israel's and Judah's sins!

> And they left all the commandments of the LORD their God, and made them molten images, *even* two calves, and made a grove, and worshipped all the host of heaven, and served Baal. And they caused their sons and their daughters to pass through the fire, and used divination and enchantments, and sold themselves to do evil in the sight of the LORD, to provoke him to anger. Therefore the LORD was very angry with Israel, and removed them out of his sight: there was none left but the tribe of Judah only. Also Judah kept not the commandments of the LORD their God, but walked in the statutes of Israel which they made. (2Kings 17:16-19)

Israel and Judah (Jews) fell under condemnation for the terrible sins they committed against God Almighty and found themselves subject to severe judgment. The 9th chapter of the book of Daniel describes the time frame for

God's judgment and the reason for this condemnation which is upon mankind. Daniel wrote that 70 weeks had been decreed against the people and upon the holy city, which is Jerusalem. The decree was a declaration of judgment. The sentence was for a period of time equaling 480 years. The word seven in Hebrew (H4760-shabua) doesn't just refer to our understanding of a week's period of time. It specifically means weeks of years, thus 480 years. God determined this length of time to put an end to sins, to make reconciliation for iniquity (judgment), to bring in everlasting righteousness, and to complete the prophet's vision by anointing Jesus as Messiah and King (Daniel 9:24).

God is dealing with the elimination of all sin from the earth, which will occur with the elimination of the sinner. It should be understood that God's wrath or judgment during the "Great Tribulation" is upon all those who are under condemnation because of their sin.

Daniel continues his prophecy by saying from the time of the commandment to restore and to rebuild Jerusalem, after it was destroyed by the Babylonians, unto the time of Messiah the prince was a period of 69 weeks of years (69x7) or 483 years (Daniel 9:25). The "Grace Period" started after the death, burial and resurrection of Jesus Christ and at the pouring out of the Holy Spirit on Pentecost. There is a parenthesis of time where God's judgment is suspended. The "Church Age" or "Grace Period" gives everyone during that time, Jew and Gentile, the opportunity to find salvation and be delivered from the coming judgment for sin. Jews today have to come to faith in Jesus the Messiah in order to avoid God's judgment. The church age will come to its end and the final 7 years of Daniel's 70 sevens prophecy will begin. The "Great Tribulation" will start with Jesus opening the 1st seal judgment (Revelation 6:1).

God offers a covenant relationship with mankind and shows how serious this relationship is as he seals the New Testament (Covenant) in the blood of His son Jesus.

How much more shall the blood of Christ, who through the eternal Spirit offered himself without spot to God, purge your conscience from dead works to serve the living God? And for this cause he is the mediator of the new testament, that by means of death, for the redemption of the transgressions *that were* under the first testament, they which are called might receive the promise of eternal inheritance. (Hebrews 9:14-15)

The Old Testament prophets spoke of a time at the end of the age when there would be a great day of judgment from the Lord. Here are just a few scriptures to verify the coming retribution:

Behold, the day of the LORD cometh, cruel both with wrath and fierce anger, to lay the land desolate: and <u>he shall destroy the sinners thereof out of it</u>. (Isaiah 13:9) Not Saints!

Alas for the day! for the day of the LORD *is* at hand, and as a <u>destruction from the Almighty</u> shall it come. (Joel 1:15)

The great day of the LORD *is* near, *it is* near, and hasteth greatly, *even* the voice of the day of the LORD: the mighty man shall cry there bitterly. (Zephaniah 1:14)

Proclaim ye this among the Gentiles; Prepare war, wake up the mighty men, let all the men of war draw near; let them come up: (Joel 3:9)

It only takes a little study with a concordance or a computer and a person can find many Old Testament scriptures plainly telling the reader that God is going to judge this world because of sin and mankind's unwillingness to believe on Him! But what about the believer who has said yes to Jesus Christ and has been born again from above?

Why would a person believe that God will purposefully allow people who have committed their lives to Him to be subject to the end time judgment of sinners who are out of the will of God? I have heard people say that "God will save the church through the tribulation". Revelation 6:8 and 9:18 are warnings to mankind that at least ½ of the world's population are going to be killed during this 7 year period. The scriptures do not give an account of the numbers of people who would otherwise be maimed or in some way injured.

God has set a precedent in the earth that he will not judge the righteous with the wicked. Before the world wide flood of Noah's day God saw that people were wicked and their hearts were only evil continually (Genesis 6:5). The bible tells us that it "repenteth" God that He made them. At that time the earth was corrupt before God and filled with violence (Genesis 6:11 and 12). The conditions on earth today are comparable to Noah's day!

God was totally disgusted with the sin of humanity and decided to destroy man whom he had created (Genesis 6:7), but <u>Noah found "Grace"</u> (Genesis 6:8) because he was just and walked with the Lord. God gave Noah instructions to build an ark so that when the flood came upon the earth Noah and his family could be saved from the imminent judgment. When the flood came only 8 souls out of the earth's population of that day were saved. Noah, Shem, Ham, Japheth and their wives were spared (Genesis 7:13-21). Take note that Noah and his family were not protected through the judgment but they were raised above the judgment in the "ark" of safety.

It was a similar situation with Lot and his family, who lived in Sodom (Genesis 14:12) in the day when firey judgment was to rain down upon Sodom and Gomorrah and the cities of the plain. The men of Sodom were exceedingly wicked (Genesis 13:13). The Lord said that the sins of Sodom and Gomorrah were grievous in his sight (Genesis 18:20) and it is recorded that the men of Sodom tried to capture 2 angels, who appeared as men, for the purpose of their immoral desires (Genesis 19:4-8). The 2 angels warned Lot of the pending judgment that would come on Sodom and Gomorrah and instructed him to take his family and leave. Lot's son-in-laws would not leave the city as they were most likely caught up in the immorality. The angels took Lot, his wife and daughters and led them out of the city because Lot had found "grace" with the Lord (Genesis 19:18-19). One angel told them to hurry and get out of Sodom for he could do nothing until they were clear of the area (Genesis 19:22). The morning Lot and his daughters entered Zoar the Lord rained fire and brimstone down upon Sodom and Gomorrah (Genesis 19:19-24). Once again God shows those who find "Grace" will not be judged with the wicked. God does not force the righteous to survive the judgment He brings upon the wicked, He removes them from the danger!

The "Great Tribulation" will occur. It is just a matter of God's timing! Many say the "Great Tribulation" is the last 3 ½ years after the peace treaty is broken by the Antichrist. This is probably based on the passage in Revelation 7:14 concerning those who were in white robes that were identified as coming out of great tribulation. Lest we forget, the lamb opens the 1st seal in Revelation 6:1. This is the start of the 7 years of judgment and as the years progress the conditions on earth get extremely bad.

In Revelation 6:1 the white horse appears to be carrying the man of sin (antichrist) into the end time scenario with his phony peace treaty (1st Seal). The 2nd rider is on a red horse and he takes away peace from earth through tremendous wars that will kill multitudes (2nd Seal). The 3rd rider on the black horse has a pair of scales measuring the cost of food, which pictures death through famine (3rd Seal). The 4th rider, death, is on a pale or puss colored horse and death follows him (4th Seal). The horses and riders signify the extreme amount of death which occurs on earth through wars, famine and the resulting plagues (Revelation 6:1-8). This carnage all happens before the trumpet or bowl judgments listed later in the book of Revelation. Verse #6:8 tells us that by the end of the 4th seal judgment one quarter of the earth's population (over 1.5 billion) has been killed with sword, and with hunger, and with death, and with the beasts of the earth". There are still 3 more seals to be opened before the 7 seals are finished.

The middle of the tribulation period appears to be described in Revelation chapters 10-12. How can anyone believe that God who is known to be "Love" will allow his children who have presented their lives to Him as living sacrifices (Romans 12:1-2) to be subject to the massacre that will take place in just these early stages of the tribulation period that lasts 7 years.

There are many Old Testament scriptures that reassure the New Testament saints that they have the opportunity to avoid this end time judgment if they are right with God. Here are a few of them:

Psalm 50:4-5 He shall call to the heavens from above, and to the earth, that he may judge his people. **<u>Gather my saints together unto me; those that have made a covenant with me by sacrifice.</u>**

Joel 2:15-16 the trumpet in Zion, sanctify a fast, call a solemn assembly: **<u>Gather the people</u>**, sanctify the congregation, assemble the elders, gather the children, and those that suck the breasts: **<u>let the bridegroom go forth of his chamber, and the bride out of her closet</u>**.

Zephaniah 2:1-3 **<u>Gather yourselves together</u>**, yea, gather together, O nation not desired; Before the decree bring forth, before the day pass as the chaff, before the fierce anger of the LORD come upon you, **<u>before the day of the LORD'S anger come upon you</u>**. Seek ye the LORD, all ye meek of the earth, which have wrought his judgment; seek righteousness, seek meekness: **<u>it may be ye shall be hid in the day of the LORD'S anger</u>**.

Isaiah 26:2 Open ye the gates, that the righteous nation which keepeth the truth may enter in.

Isaiah 26:19-21 Thy dead men shall live (Old Covenant dead), together with my dead body shall they arise (New Covenant dead). Awake and sing, ye that dwell in dust: for thy dew is as the dew of herbs, and the earth shall cast out the dead. **Come, my people** (saints alive on earth), enter thou into thy chambers, and shut thy doors about thee: **hide thyself as it were for a little moment, until the indignation be overpast.** For, behold, <u>the LORD cometh out of his place to punish the inhabitants of the earth for their iniquity</u>: the earth also shall disclose her blood, and shall no more cover her slain.

The New Testament scriptures contain further reasons to believe in the rapture doctrine. It is difficult to make another person see what they do not want to acknowledge, however the preponderance of evidence for a pre-trib rapture is hard to ignore. Let's look at some New Testament reasons for a pre-trib rapture.

The Apostle Paul wrote to the church in Thessalonica letting them know that at the end of this dispensation those who were still alive in Christ could not delay or prevent the resurrection of those that were already dead in Christ. Paul described the event by saying that the Lord Jesus himself will descend from heaven with the sound of a trumpet and the dead in Christ shall be raised. Those who are alive shall be caught up with those raised from the dead and together all will meet the Lord Jesus in the air. Those who are a part of this resurrection have the promise of being with Jesus forever (1 Thessalonians 4:15-18). At this point the word of God does not say Jesus comes to earth!

In these scriptures it is apparent that there is going to be a resurrection from the dead and that those who are in Christ Jesus will be "caught up" in the air to meet Jesus. The word caught up in the Greek is harpazō and means to catch away or up, to pluck, to seize or take by force. This word gives us understanding that the saints of God are removed with haste. Most assuredly the saints are being removed from the danger to come?

1 Thessalonians 4:15-18 is similar to the Apostle Paul's letter to the church in Corinth. Paul is sharing understanding of a great mystery telling saints that in a moment, in the twinkling of an eye, at the last trumpet sound the dead shall be raised incorruptible and those who are alive in Christ shall be changed from

mortal to immortal. Actually Paul writes that the natural body is corruptible subject to destruction and it must be changed to incorruption, which is eternal life. The true believer will one day put on immortality (1 Corinthians 15:51-53).

In both of these previously mentioned sets of scriptures we are given to understand that there will be a resurrection of dead saints and that there will be a change in the bodies of the living saints. The change from mortal to immortality is in the preparation for a different dimension that the saved will be living. Flesh and blood cannot inherit the kingdom of God (1 Corinthians 15:50).

The true church is preparing to leave planet earth until the punishment for sin has ceased (Isaiah 26:20). God's fury is going to be poured out on those who will not accept the free gift of life and right standing with God. But if we examine ourselves and make proper decisions for our lives in Christ we will not be judged or condemned with the world (1 Corinthians 11:28-32).

The Apostle Peter wrote, "For the time is come that judgment must begin at the house of God: and if *it* first begin at us, what shall the end *be* of them that obey not the gospel of God? And if the righteous scarcely (with much effort) be saved, where shall the ungodly and the sinner appear? Wherefore let them that suffer according to the will of God commit the keeping of their souls to him in well doing, as unto a faithful Creator (1 Peter 4:17-19)".

The book of Revelation is set up in such a way that if we just consider the progression of events and what is being declared we have a good look into the future. This book is actually the "Revelation of Jesus Christ", which God gave to him! Jesus sent the message to John through an angel so that the end time scenario might be understood (Revelation 1:1). Chapters 2 and 3 are addressed to the 7 churches that were in Asia (modern Turkey), but they have relevance to each of 7 distinct periods that the church at large experiences through the "Grace Period".

When the Apostle John wrote the book of Revelation he recorded what he had experienced in the spirit. He wrote that a door was opened in heaven and the 1st voice he heard was like a trumpet inviting him to come up. He was told that he was going to be shown things that must come to pass (Revelation 4:1). John wrote that immediately he was in heaven and saw a throne with someone setting on it. Based on the description, it had to be God. John described many of the things he saw in heaven including 24 elders who were seated (Revelation 4:3-11). In the 5th chapter John saw a book in the right hand of God who was sitting on the throne. The book had 7 seals. John wrote that he wept because no one was worthy to open this book. One of the elders informed John that the "Lion of the Tribe of Judah" had prevailed and was worthy to open the book. His attention was drawn to "A Lamb As If It Had Been Slain" who then took the book from God. The 24 elders began to sing. Attention has to be paid to what they were singing because it identifies those singing! They were singing, "Thou art worthy to take the book, and to open the seals thereof: for thou wast slain, and hast redeemed us to God by thy blood out of every kindred, and tongue, and people, and nation; And hast made us unto our God kings and priests: and we shall reign on the earth (Revelation 5:1-10)." The one who is worthy can only refer to Jesus Christ! Jesus has redeemed the souls of true believers through his blood sacrifice on the cross of Calvary! No doubt the 24 elders are the resurrected patriarchs from the 12 tribes of Israel (Old Covenant) and the 12 apostles (New Covenant). Obviously there are more than just the 24 people singing because those gathered there are the saved out of every family, tongue, people and nation.

Revelation chapter 6:1 begins with the opening of the 1st seal, which begins the judgment of God upon humanity. In chapter 5 the elders represent the resurrected and raptured saints of God. Just as the scriptures have said there will be those who are saved from the judgment that is coming! **How can a person imagine that Jesus would give his life for people, see them saved and then commence judgment on the unbeliever without first securing the safety of his children?**

The picture here gives us great confidence of a pre-trib rapture of the true church. Many will say that the rapture theories only began within the last few hundred years. The word of God lets us know it has been in the plan of God from the foundation of the world.

The Feasts of Israel also suggest to us that God is employing the Old Covenant to help us understand what He is doing through Christ. In the 23rd chapter of Leviticus God gives instruction to Israel for preservation and celebration of 7 holy convocations or feasts. All 7 celebrations were rehearsals for the coming Messiah. The first 4 feasts are the Passover (Jesus is our Passover Lamb), the Feast of Unleavened Bread (holiness through Christ's example), the Feast of First Fruits (Jesus is the first fruits of the resurrection) and Pentecost (Jesus poured out his spirit/life on this feast day to those in the upper room and the church age begins). There is a space of time between the spring feasts and the fall feasts. The gap represents the time period of the harvest when the crop is growing to maturity ("Grace Period"). The 1st 4 feasts speak of Jesus' first coming.

The last 3 feasts give us a picture of Jesus' 2nd coming! The 5th feast is the Jewish New Year called Rosh Hashanah or "head of the year". This feast is also called the Feast of Trumpets and is a 2 day celebration. It is a high holy day to the Jews. At the end of the grace period when the last trumpet blasts the dead in Christ will rise (includes OT saints), the true saints of God who are alive will be changed. They will all meet Jesus in the air to be with him forever! This all happens before the "Great Tribulation".

The Day of Atonement is the 6th feast and it is a picture of the atonement for sin. On this day the high priest of Israel would take the blood sacrifice in the Holy of Holies as specified in the Mosaic Law and offer it upon the Mercy Seat. God required this sacrifice under the Old Covenant as a covering for sins. Under the New Covenant, if the blood of Jesus has not been applied to the life of a living person for the atonement or forgiveness of their sins, that individual will have to pay the penalty themselves. All those who are alive on earth at this time will experience the "Great Tribulation" where God finally puts an end to sin as was discussed in Daniel chapter 9!

The 7th feast is the "Feast of Tabernacles", which speaks of the 1,000 year reign of Jesus Christ on earth.

All these signs point to the soon return of the Lord Jesus and many people acknowledge this to be true. What will happen 1st? It appears clear to many that God will send his son Jesus to secure his family and take them to safety.

Then there will be "Great Tribulation" like that which has never been seen before! I pray you are one of God's children!

Chapter 9

A WOMAN AND A SCARLET COLORED BEAST

There has never in world history existed anything like the "American Experiment", people governing themselves! Throughout time, we have seen many types of governments come and go, but nothing like the United States of America. No other government has ever been established of the people, by the people or for the people as Abraham Lincoln so apply stated!

During the days of Nebuchadnezzar the world witnessed the first real world government, which was a totalitarian form of control over the people. Babylon was said to have been a glorious place with walls chariots could race upon. The hanging gardens were considered to be one of the seven wonders of the ancient world. But still, one man ruled the civilized world.

In Nebuchadnezzar's dream, he sees a colossus, a giant, which illustrates Gentile world government (Daniel chapter 2). When reading Daniel's account of the dream the reader notes that the various empires are represented with metallic values; fine gold, silver, bronze and iron. Close observation tells us that the value of the metal decreases, while at the same time the metal gets increasingly harder. Daniel makes known that Babylon under Nebuchadnezzar is the head of fine gold. It is a dictatorship in a time of spears and arrows.

Over time, the Roman Empire becomes dominant in the world and is portrayed as iron. The Roman Empire was governed by a Caesar and a senate. The degradation of the metal pictures the reduction of authority from an autocracy or monarchy to a democracy, which allows for a representative form of government.

Also, with the progression of time, weaponry becomes more sophisticated and militaries come to be more ferocious.

As we again look at Nebuchadnezzar's dream, we note ten toes on the colossus made of iron and clay (Daniel 2:33). If the lesser values in the different metals is a reflection of the reduction of authoritative control from a dictatorship to a democracy, what must the clay represent if not anarchy? Clay, even if dry, does not compare to the hardness or consistency of iron. The clay and iron are not cohesive. At the end of Gentile dominance in the world, there must be chaos as a powerful world authority ("One World Government") fights off pockets of resistance. Clay and iron do not bond!

Well where are we? History and current events come together to let us all know that we are approaching the end of an era, a course correction for humanity, yes a "New World Order". It is not the "New World Order" the politicians are talking about, though that will come at the very end of Gentile world rule under the "Antichrist". The course correction the bible speaks of is when a stone hits the colossus in the feet and the iron, the clay, the brass, the silver, and the gold are broken to pieces together and become like the chaff of the summer threshing floors where the wind carries them away, that no place is found for them (Daniel 2:35).

The "New World Order" the bible speaks of is the Kingdom of God, which is a theocracy with Jesus, the anointed of God, sitting on his throne in Jerusalem. Until that time, we are faced with current events and the unfolding of a diabolical attempt to destroy the "American Experiment", which is self-governing by the people of this United States of America. The USA is under attack by enemies both foreign and domestic. The history books, encyclopedias and the Internet are replete with various creditable sources, which lay out the plans of evil men and women who would have the United States lose its sovereignty to the United Nations and their "New World Order".

There are many who believe that the United States of America is not mentioned in God's word. Of course we wouldn't expect to see the "USA" named as such in the bible. It did not exist then, and none of the prophets would have known it by name. Even though they were led by the Holy Spirit, the prophets did not always understand what they saw or heard by the Spirit of God. They just recorded what they were given. Can anyone imagine that the most prosperous nation and the greatest military power to this time would not be spoken of by the prophets in some form or fashion within God's word?

When we think about the power and ability of mankind, we are reminded of the tower of Babel. Remember that the whole earth was of one language and of one speech. As they began to build the tower, the word of God says that, "nothing will be restrained from them, which they have imagined to do" (Genesis 11:6). What was their motivation for what they were doing? God's word says, "let us build us a city and a tower, whose top may reach unto heaven; and let us make us a name (Genesis 11:4)". Man's goal has not changed throughout time. The focus is still *self*, "let us build", "let us make us a name". As a result of man's pride and arrogance, God confounded their language, that they could not understand one another's speech, and scattered them abroad over the face of the earth.

After the invention of the printing press and the ability for man to read the "Good Book", there shown a light of reformation. What made Columbus believe that the world was not flat? Maybe it was the "written word" which told him that God is seated upon the *circle* of the earth (Isaiah 40:22). The Protestant Reformation ultimately resulted in the discovery of the "New World of the Americas". In 1620, the first settlers arrived from Plymouth England (English speaking pilgrims from the "Old World") searching for a place free from tyranny and that would enable them to worship as their conscience saw fit. Today, the USA has gathered to its shores people of every nationality and every tongue. The USA is metaphorically, if not spiritually, a modern Babylon.

It took the pilgrims months to cross the Pacific Ocean in a sail boat, but through the imagination of men like the Wright brothers, we can fly across the Atlantic in just a few hours. Think of the many inventions which have been accomplished by men and women working together, many nations or ethnicities as one, the USA. The God given brilliance of mankind, made in His image, has ignited the world and brought all its nationalities together, through the English language, in the USA. The problem however is still the same: "let us build"; "let us make us a name".

Over the last two centuries, the USA has grown from a fledgling nation to the dominating super power of the world. Our currency became the "World Reserve Currency" that all the nations of the world trade in. The USA has seen prosperity beyond belief while most of the world is still trying to come to America to be a partaker in "the dream". The life style of the now shrinking middle class in America has been the envy of the rest of the world for decades. However, America's arrogance and disrespect for other nations has, over time, been recognized abroad! The USA is now hated by many nations and has even become a target for terrorists.

What then is the future of the USA, and where can we see America in the scriptures? If the USA is not named in the bible, it is, without question, depicted or illustrated throughout many scriptures. Following are some things to consider.

The USA is a progeny of England. In 1776, the USA rebelled against King George III of England and declared her independence. At one time, it was said that the sun never set on the British Empire. The 13 colonies of the "New World" later became the USA, which was just one of England's many territories. In Ezekiel 38:13, the mention of the "merchants of Tarshish" is a reference to traders that came from the area of "Tarshish" or "the land of tin." Many if not most scholars today believe that this is the area of present-day England. The "young lions" that come after the "merchants of Tarshish" in Ezekiel 38:13 would include America, the offspring of England, as well as Australia, Canada, and other nations that England gave birth to.

> Jeremiah 50:12 Your mother shall be sore confounded; she that bare you shall be ashamed: behold, the hindermost of the nations *shall be* a wilderness, a dry land, and a desert.

Ezekiel 38:13 Sheba, and Dedan, and the merchants of Tarshish, with all the <u>young lions thereof</u>, shall say unto thee, Art thou come to take a spoil? hast thou gathered thy company to take a prey? to carry away silver and gold, to take away cattle and goods, to take a great spoil?

The continental United States of America is bordered on the east coast by the Atlantic Ocean, on the west coast by the Pacific Ocean and on the south partially by the Gulf of Mexico. The 49th state, Alaska, is bordered by the Bering Sea, Artic Ocean & Pacific Ocean; and the 50th state, Hawaii, is surrounded by the Pacific Ocean. Consider the USA's protectorates! Puerto Rico is surrounded by the Atlantic Ocean, and Guam is surrounded by the Pacific Ocean.

Jeremiah 51:13 O <u>thou that dwellest upon many waters, abundant in treasures,</u> thine end is come, *and* the measure of thy covetousness.

Ezekiel 27:2-4 Now, thou son of man, take up a lamentation for Tyrus; And say unto Tyrus, <u>O thou that art situate at the entry of the sea, *which art* a merchant of the people for many isles,</u> Thus saith the Lord GOD; O Tyrus, thou hast said, I *am* of perfect beauty. Thy borders *are* <u>in the midst of the seas,</u> thy builders have perfected thy beauty.

Revelation 17:1 And there came one of the seven angels which had the seven vials, and talked with me, saying unto me, Come hither; I will shew unto thee the judgment of <u>the great whore that sitteth upon many waters:</u>

The most delicious foods and beverages, the most expensive goods and services are available to just about anyone who can buy or charge them through credit. Through purchasing or financing, citizens of the USA have been able to live in very nice homes, drive expensive cars and obtain their hearts desire. If it exists, whatever is wanted has been available in the USA.

Ezekiel 27:12 & 33 Tarshish *was* thy merchant by reason of the <u>multitude of</u> <u>all *kind of* riches</u>; with silver, iron, tin, and lead, they traded in thy fairs. … When thy wares went forth out of the seas, <u>thou filledst many people; thou</u> <u>didst enrich the kings of the earth</u> with the multitude of thy riches and of thy merchandise.

Ezekiel 28:16 By the multitude of thy merchandise they have <u>filled the midst of</u> <u>thee with violence, and thou hast sinned</u>: therefore I will cast thee as profane out of the mountain of God: and I will destroy thee, O covering cherub, from the midst of the stones of fire.

Revelation 18:3 For all nations have drunk of the wine of the wrath of her fornication, and <u>the kings of the earth have committed fornication with her</u>, and the merchants of the earth are waxed rich through the abundance of her delicacies.

Revelation 18:12-14 The merchandise of gold, and silver, and precious stones, and of pearls, and fine linen, and purple, and silk, and scarlet, and all thyine wood, and all manner vessels of ivory, and all manner vessels of most precious wood, and of brass, and iron, and marble, … And cinnamon, and odours, and ointments, and frankincense, and wine, and oil, and fine flour, and wheat, and beasts, and sheep, and horses, and chariots, and slaves, and souls of men. … And <u>the fruits that thy soul lusted after are departed from thee</u>, and all things which were dainty and goodly are departed from thee, and thou shalt find them no more at all.

The USA is said to be the largest producer of porn in the world. The demand for marijuana and other drugs is at an epidemic proportion. Adultery, fornication, homosexuality and abortion are made light of on TV, in movies and in other media. Unfortunately for the world, the USA has sent its missionaries and popular preachers throughout the world with a watered down message of Jesus Christ, having corrupted the gospel message through their lies and lightness (Jeremiah 23:32), with a hope of their financial gain. Many promise salvation to others but make their proselytes two fold the children of hell than they themselves (Matthew 23:15).

> Ezekiel 28:15-16 Thou *wast* perfect (H8549-upright or sound) in thy ways from the day that thou wast created (H1254-dispatched or selected), till iniquity (H5766-unrighteousness or wickedness) was found in thee. By the multitude of thy merchandise they have filled the midst of thee with violence (H2555-injustice or by figure of speech, unjust gain), and thou hast sinned: therefore I will cast thee as profane out of the mountain (H2022 – sometimes used figuratively promotion or place of authority) of God: and I will destroy thee, O covering cherub (H5526-protecting or defending H3742-imaginary figure, but remember the cherubims with the flaming swords who kept Adam and Eve out of the Garden of Eden), from the midst of the stones of fire. (One must read chapters 27 & 28 in context-it is not about a fallen angel.)

> Jeremiah 51:17-18 Every man is brutish (H1197-eaten up or wasted) by *his* knowledge; every founder is confounded (H3001-ashamed or disappointed) by the graven image: for his molten image *is* falsehood, and *there is* no breath in them. They *are* vanity, the work of errors: in the time of their visitation they shall perish.

> Revelation 17:2 & 4 With whom the kings of the earth have committed fornication, and the inhabitants of the earth have been made drunk with the wine of her fornication. … And the woman was arrayed in purple and scarlet colour, and decked with gold and precious stones and pearls, having a golden cup in her hand full of abominations and filthiness of her fornication (G4202 - spiritually idolatry).

Many leaders of the USA deny the existence of Jehovah God Creator, and have given themselves over to humanistic philosophies. They deny the God who creates through intelligent design, and offer up a big bang and primordial slime. Everyone should know that if it all started with a big bang, someone had to have lit the match! Instead of allowing God to have His way throughout American society, leadership in the USA has, through executive orders, legislation and courthouse rulings, worked to reduce Godly influence by the legalization of abortion and homosexuality. At the same time, the "Ten Commandments" and Christian symbols have been taken down from schools, court rooms and other governmental offices. Many who would ordinarily have been in support of righteousness have been silenced with a fear of litigation. Those leaders, and the people that support their ungodly views, have said to God that His will means nothing to them and promote themselves above God and His word.

From the onset of the "American Experiment", the USA, has been under attack from forces inside and outside of its government, from those who desire her destruction.

Whether anyone wants to believe it or not, the USA, according to the scriptures, must be reduced from power before a "One World Government" is able to come on the scene! The sovereignty of the USA is being destroyed! Due to the USA's controlling influence over other nations, especially in Europe, many hate her and are working behind the scenes to see her fall. Researching Fabian Socialism, Saul Alinsky and the "Cloward and Piven Strategy" will awaken most people.

God's word describes a Babylon that will appear on the scene in the last days. Many prophecy scholars believe that Iraq will rise to a position of great power in the last days in fulfillment of those scriptures. By all indications, we are in the last days. Most people believe or at least express an uneasy feeling, that this might be true. It is difficult to imagine that once again, at this late date, Iraq could rise to become a great world power. There is not enough time!

As you review the following scriptures, consider a spiritual application to that of Babylon, that "Great City Babylon" and quite possibly the USA:

Isaiah 14:4 … thou shalt take up this proverb against the king of Babylon, and say, How hath the oppressor ceased! the golden city ceased!

Isaiah 21:9 … behold, here cometh a chariot of men, *with* a couple of horsemen. And he answered and said, Babylon is fallen, is fallen; and all the graven images of her gods he hath broken unto the ground.

Jeremiah 50:8-9 Remove out of the midst of Babylon, and go forth out of the land of the Chaldeans, and be as the he goats before the flocks. For, lo, I will raise and cause to come up against Babylon an assembly of great nations from the north country: and they shall set themselves in array against her; from thence she shall be taken: their arrows *shall be* as of a mighty expert man; none shall return in vain.

Jeremiah 50:32 And the most proud shall stumble and fall, and none shall raise him up: and I will kindle a fire in his cities, and it shall devour all round about him.

Jeremiah 50:46 At the noise of the taking of Babylon the earth is moved, and the cry is heard among the nations.

Jeremiah 51:7-8 Babylon *hath been* a golden cup (priceless vessel) in the LORD'S hand, that made all the earth drunken: the nations have drunken of her wine; therefore the nations are mad. Babylon is suddenly fallen and destroyed: howl for her; take balm for her pain, if so be she may be healed.

Jeremiah 51:13 O thou that dwellest upon many waters, abundant in treasures, thine end is come, *and* the measure of thy covetousness.

Jeremiah 51:58 Thus saith the LORD of hosts; The broad walls (defences) of Babylon shall be utterly broken, and her high gates shall be burned with fire; and the people shall labour in vain, and the folk in the fire, and they shall be weary.

Ezekiel 27:34-36 In the time *when* <u>thou shalt be broken by the seas in the depths of the waters</u> thy merchandise and all thy company in the midst of thee shall fall. All the inhabitants of the isles shall be astonished at thee, and their kings shall be sore afraid, they shall be troubled in *their* countenance. The merchants among the people shall hiss at thee; thou shalt be a terror, and never *shalt be* any more.

Revelation 14:8 And there followed another angel, saying, Babylon is fallen, is fallen, that great city, because she made all nations drink of the wine of the wrath of her fornication.

Revelation 17:3-4 So he carried me away in the spirit into the wilderness: and I saw <u>a woman sit upon a scarlet coloured beast, full of names of blasphemy</u>, having seven heads and ten horns. And the woman was arrayed in purple and scarlet colour, and decked with gold and precious stones and pearls, having <u>a golden cup in her hand full of abominations and filthiness of her fornication</u>:

Revelation 17:15 And he saith unto me, <u>The waters</u> which thou sawest, where the whore sitteth (G2521 - sitteth: dwell or remain), <u>are peoples, and multitudes, and nations, and tongues</u>.

Revelation 17:16 And <u>the ten horns</u> which thou sawest upon the beast, these shall <u>hate the whore</u>, and shall make her desolate and naked, and shall eat her flesh, and burn her with fire.

Revelation 18:4 And I heard another voice from heaven, saying, Come out of her, my people, that ye be not partakers of her sins, and that ye receive not of her plagues.

Revelation 18:8 Therefore shall her plagues come in one day, death, and mourning, and famine; and she shall be utterly burned with fire: for strong *is* the Lord God who judgeth her.

Revelation 18:9-11 And the kings of the earth, who have committed fornication and lived deliciously with her, shall bewail her, and lament for her, when they shall see the smoke of her burning, Standing afar off for the fear of her torment, saying, Alas, alas, that great city Babylon, that mighty city! for in one hour is thy judgment come. And the merchants of the earth shall weep and mourn over her; for no man buyeth their merchandise any more:

Do we accept and believe the truth of scripture or do we hold to tradition? Satan has, through tradition, corrupted the gospel message and thereby destroyed the power of the word to transform our society into God fearing people. God's judgment must, and will, come to the USA. God is not a man that he would declare a word and not uphold it, neither is He the son of man that he will pity humanity for their lack of faith and change his mind (Numbers 23:19)

We read in Genesis 6:5-7 that God observed the actions of the human race and declared, through His word, that the people were very wicked. He stated that every concept or purpose within their thoughts was nothing but evil all the time. God regretted that he had made man on the earth, and He was sore vexed. Jehovah decided to destroy man whom He created; "both man, and beast, and the creeping thing, and the fowls of the air"; for He lamented that He had made them. God caused a great flood upon the earth. His righteous judgment destroyed the human race except for Noah and his family. Genesis 6:8 tells us

<u>Noah found grace</u>! The population of the earth, in that day, was destroyed except for 8 individuals of one family.

Another family in the bible found salvation in the day God's judgment came upon Sodom and Gomorrah, in the days of Abraham. Lot, the nephew of Abram (Abraham), left his homeland when Abram departed for the land of promise. Through the course of events, Lot and his family found themselves living in Sodom. The apostle Peter lets us know that Lot was a righteous man vexed with the filth of the wicked, 2 Peter 2:7-8. However, Genesis 18:20 says that the sin of the people in Sodom and Gomorrah was very grievous. In the following chapter, Genesis 19:24, we read that God rained fire down upon Sodom and Gomorrah. Scripture states that God's judgment upon Sodom and Gomorrah could only happened after Lot and his family departed out of the cities and away from judgment. Lots two son in-laws would not leave, and they were destroyed. As Lot, his wife and their two daughters were leaving Sodom, Lot's wife looked back and became a pillar of salt. She also received God's judgment. Jesus gives warning instructing believers to remember Lot's wife. Christians must not look back on their old lives with fond desire for the things they have left behind!

Whether all, or none, of the prophetic scriptures shared apply to the United States of America, for only time will tell, there is little doubt God's judgment is coming upon planet earth and upon the USA. God's wrath will finally be realized by a world gone mad in iniquity. Only those in right standing with God through Christ Jesus will be spared. There is a preponderance of evidence!

TIME IS RUNNING OUT!

Y
JUST A COUPLE OF THINGS

The word of God tells us to study to show ourselves approved unto God. There are areas of biblical discussion that need to be studied to rightly divide God's word (2 Timothy 2:15). There will be 2 considered here.

There are scriptures in the King James Bible that have been translated to say that the worlds were made by Jesus. Did Jesus himself speak the worlds into being? What does the word of God really say? Let's look at 2 scriptures:

Colossians 1:14-17 … we have redemption through his (Jesus') blood, *even* the forgiveness of sins: (15) Who is the image of the invisible God, the firstborn of every creature: (16) For by (G1722) him were all things created, that are in heaven, and that are in earth, visible and invisible, whether *they be* thrones, or dominions, or principalities, or powers: all things were created by (G1223 because of) him, and for him: (17) And he is before all things, and by (G1223 because of) him all things consist (were made).

Hebrews 1:1-2 God, who at sundry times and in divers manners spake in time past unto the fathers by the prophets, (2) Hath in these last days spoken unto us by *his* Son, whom he hath appointed heir of all things, by (G1223) whom also he made the worlds;

Please note in both the above scriptures the use of the word "by". Here are the definitions of the 2 words translated "by" from the Greek:

G1722 εν en *en* A primary preposition denoting (fixed) *position* (in place, time or state), and (by implication) *instrumentality* (medially or constructively), that is, **a relation of *rest*** (intermediate between <u>G1519</u> and <u>G1537</u>); *"in"*, *at*, (up-) *on, by*, etc.: - about, after, against, + almost, X altogether, among, X as, at, before, between, (here-) **by** (+ all means), **for (. . . sake of),** + give self wholly to, (here-) in (-to, -wardly), X mightily, **(because) of,** (up-) on, [open-] ly, X outwardly, one, X quickly, X shortly, [speedi-] ly, X that, X there (-in, -on), **through** (-out), (un-) to(-ward), under, when, where (-with), while, with (-in).

G1223 διά dia *dee-ah'* A primary preposition denoting the *channel* of an act; *through* (in very wide applications, local, causal or occasional). In composition it retains the same general import: - after, always, among, at, to avoid, **because of** (that), briefly, **by,** for (cause) . . . fore, **from,** in, by occasion of, of, **by reason of,** for sake, that, thereby, therefore, X though, **through** (-out), to, wherefore, with (-in). In composition it retains the same general import.

Note that there are several applications of the Greek word en and dia' especially the prepositions because of, by reason of and through! We can understand then that all things were created by (because of) Jesus, and for him. Secondly, by (because of) Jesus he (God) made the worlds! It should be noted in Hebrews 1:2 that it is stated Jesus was appointed heir of all things. In Romans 8:17 it also says that the saints are to be joint heirs with Jesus. The question one must ask is how can you inherit something you made?? Obviously it was the Lord God who spoke everything into existence!

John 1:1 has gendered a considerable amount of discussion with most people interpreting the verse as stating that Jesus is God.

John 1:1 In the beginning was the <u>Word</u>, and the Word was with <u>God</u>, and the Word was <u>God</u>.

Word: **G3056** λόγος logos *log'-os*

From **G3004**; something *said* (including the *thought*); by implication a *topic* (subject of discourse), also *reasoning* (the mental faculty) or *motive*; by extension a *computation*; (inserted by Young's and not from the Greek: ~~specifically (with the article in John) the Divine *Expression* (that is, *Christ*)~~ - account, cause, communication, X concerning, doctrine, fame, X have to do, intent, matter, mouth, preaching, question, reason, + reckon, remove, say (-ing), shew, X speaker, speech, talk, thing, + none of these things move me, tidings, treatise, utterance, word, work.

God: **G2316** θεός theos *theh'-os*

Of uncertain affinity; a *deity*, especially (with **G3588**) **the** supreme *Divinity*; figuratively a *magistrate*; by Hebraism *very:* - X exceeding, God, **god [-ly,** -ward].

There is no pure Greek translation that indicates the word "word" can be translated to mean Jesus. In the beginning was the word (reason or motive) and the word was with God (the supreme divinity-noun) and the word was God (godly or divine-adjective). Note the different spellings in the Greek language.

97

John 1:1	John 1:14
In the commencement of the creation there was intent. The plan was God's mental faculty and the reasoning was divine!	The plan of God centered around His son became reality to the creation when Jesus was born! We perceive the glory of God upon him.

There are many traditions that have been passed down over the last 2 centuries that need to be examined much closer. We have to make our calling and elections sure!

Z
FINAL COMMENTS

2 Timothy 3:16-17 <u>All scripture</u> *is* given by inspiration of God, and *is* <u>profitable for doctrine</u>, for reproof, for correction, for instruction in righteousness: That the man of God may be perfect, throughly furnished unto all good works.

2 Peter 1:19-21 We have also a more sure word of prophecy; whereunto ye do well that ye take heed, as unto a light that shineth in a dark place, until the day dawn, and the day star arise in your hearts: Knowing this first, that <u>no prophecy of the scripture is of any private interpretation</u>. For the prophecy came not in old time by the will of man: but <u>holy men of God spake *as they were* moved by the Holy Ghost</u>.

Salvation is a personal thing and eternal life must be received by each of us individually according to the will of God. I would ask the reader to think back to the "Tabernacle in the Wilderness". There is a process whereby we must approach the throne of God and have access into His kingdom. We cannot claim a birth right into God's family based on our personal beliefs. The course for humanity has been laid out. There must be a sacrifice of self through repentance, which means we accept God's way for our lives. This will require that we give up our own opinions and traditions. There must be cleansing through waters of baptism in Jesus' name according to the gospel preached by the apostles. We then enter the "Holy Place" through the infilling of the Holy

Spirit, which is new life from the Lord. Only then do we have access to God, who invites us to come boldly unto His throne of grace! Please pray about what you have read and ask God for wisdom and faith to understand in the face of tradition!

ABOUT THE AUTHOR

Bishop Jim has been married to his wife, Cathy, for forty-six years. They have four children and nine grandchildren. They were both saved in 1974. God immediately placed a hunger in Jim's spirit to understand and share God's word. Jim was called to the ministry the following year and has had the honor of pastoring since 1980. Jim interpreted and applied insurance coverage handling fire and casualty claims for many years. This helped him in his study of God's word. Jim was conferred the title of bishop in 2012 for his many years of faithfulness to the ministry. Jim's heart is to see people come to the knowledge of the truth and to be set free from the condemnation of sin. Bishop Jim strongly believes that those who have been blessed by God must share the good news of salvation in Jesus Christ!

Contact Information
Bishop James Disbrow
P.O. Box 72
Holly, MI. 48442
jdiz2@sbcglobal.net